O is for Outings!

OPENING CEREMONY

Est. 2002

CAROL LIM & HUMBERTO LEON

New York · Paris · London · Milan

First published in the United States of America in 2012
by Rizzoli International Publications, Inc.
300 Park Avenue South
New York, NY 10010
rizzoliusa.com

Photo stickers on book cover, Clockwise from top
right: Opening Ceremony SS12, photographed by
Tim Barber; Carol and Humberto, photographed
by Jason Frank Rothenberg; Spike Jonze photographed
by Humberto Leon; Chloë Sevigny photographed by
KT Auleta, 2010.

2012 2013 2014 2015 / 10 9 8 7 6 5 4 3 2 1

Editor: Rory Satran
Rizzoli Editors: Ken Miller and Julie Schumacher
Designer: Su Barber
Production: Kaija Markoe
Managing Editor: Anthony Petrillose

ISBN: 978-0-8478-3870-7
Library of Congress Catalog Control Number:
2012933953
Printed in China

OPENING CEREMONY

Est. 2002

HELLO!

WELCOME TO THE WORLD OF OPENING CEREMONY. OUR JOURNEY BEGAN WHEN WE MET IN COLLEGE AT THE UNIVERSITY OF CALIFORNIA AT BERKELEY, STARTED OUR CAREERS IN FASHION SEPARATELY, AND THEN IN 2002 WE OPENED A STORE TOGETHER IN DOWNTOWN NEW YORK.

OUR CONCEPT FOR OPENING CEREMONY IS TO TRAVEL TO A NEW COUNTRY EACH YEAR AND BRING BACK THE BEST OF ITS FASHION AND CULTURE. SINCE THE IDEA WAS LOOSELY BASED ON BARON de COUBERTIN'S ORIGINAL MODEL FOR THE OLYMPICS, WE CALLED IT OPENING CEREMONY.

NOW THE OPENING CEREMONY UNIVERSE INCLUDES TWO STORES IN NEW YORK CITY, A MINI-MALL IN LOS ANGELES, AN EIGHT LEVEL DEPARTMENT STORE IN TOKYO, AN E-STORE AND BLOG, A SHOWROOM, A TV CHANNEL (OCTV), AND A CLOTHING LINE THAT IS SOLD AROUND THE WORLD. WE'VE COLLABORATED WITH FRIENDS AND ARTISTS CHLOË SEVIGNY, SPIKE JONZE, KATE & LAURA MULLEAVY OF RODARTE, AUREL SCHMIDT, TERENCE KOH, AND SO MANY OTHERS.

WE'VE GONE FROM EATING DUMPLINGS AND HELPING ONLY ONE CUSTOMER IN A WHOLE DAY AT OUR HOWARD STREET SHOP TO CREATING OUR OWN WORLD THAT IS A LAUNCHING PLACE FOR EMERGING FASHION BRANDS AND CULTURE IN DOWNTOWN NEW YORK AND BEYOND. WELCOME TO TEN OF THE CRAZIEST YEARS EVER! HERE'S OUR STORY, WITH A LITTLE HELP FROM OUR FRIENDS.

XOXO,
CAROL & HUMBERTO

35 Howard Street, New York 10013 T. (212) 219-2688 F. (2
Showroom: 10 Greene Street, New York 10013 T. (212) 226-1885
www.openingceremony.us

Carol Lim and Humberto
Leon photographed by
Terry Richardson, 2011.
PREVIOUS SPREAD: Opening
Ceremony New York team
photographed by Sasha
Eisenman for *Intermission*
magazine, 2010.

What is Opening Ceremony? Pop!

ERIC WILSON

Eric Wilson has been a fashion reporter at The New York Times *since 2005. Prior to joining* The Times*, he was a reporter for* Women's Wear Daily *and columnist for* W *magazine from 1997 to 2004. He is a graduate of New York University with degrees in journalism and fine arts.*

For every generation of style-minded New Yorkers, there has been one store that managed, above all others, to crystallize a sense of fashion of the moment. In the 1960s, it was Paraphernalia, a shop on Madison Avenue and 67th Street that stayed open until midnight on Mondays, Wednesdays, and Fridays, selling the mod and mini fashions of Mary Quant, Rudi Gernreich, and Betsey Johnson. In the 1970s, it was Charivari, with multiple stores on the Upper West Side, where intellectual fashion intermingled with go-go boys and future fashion stars. (Marc Jacobs was a teenage stock boy). In the 1980s, there was Fiorucci, once described as the "daytime Studio 54" for introducing designer jeans and skintight club clothes. The designer-label-bubble of the 1990s was matched by the fast expansion of Barneys New York, from its historic Chelsea store to Madison Avenue and beyond.

Pop.

In 2002, no one could not have predicted that Opening Ceremony, a thrifty little hole in the wall on what was perhaps the last grim strip of SoHo—which was then untouched by Big Fashion—would go on to become the most influential retailer of its decade. The store did not seem so much designed as thrown together, with clothes piled on a table or placed on racks, seemingly at random. Browsing an ethnic-print jacket, or a deeply-pleated pair of pants, or some piece of fabric tied around a hanger, it wasn't entirely clear where the menswear ended and the womenswear began. The curtains of the dressing rooms, right in the middle of the store, didn't even close all the way. (They still don't.)

You also knew right away that this place was something different, a store where you never knew what to expect, other than at least one of the owners, Carol Lim or Humberto Leon, would be working on the sales floor, selling a mix of designers including some insider favorites (Proenza Schouler, Band of Outsiders, Rodarte) and some especially unfamiliar names (Moo Piyasombatkul, Arc'teryx Veilance). I once bought a

$300 pair of shorts there by a designer whose name is, evidently, a Roman numeral.

By traveling the world in search of new designers and ideas, Carol and Humberto, self-professed California mall kids weaned on Vision Streetwear and *Vision Quest*, have created a constant sense of discovery in Opening Ceremony. And they never seem exhausted, either, despite simultaneously operating a showroom; designing a house line; collaborating with a wide variety of both couture and street labels; running stores in New York, Los Angeles, and Tokyo; and, oh, becoming the creative directors of Kenzo in Paris.

Perhaps the reason they connect so well to contemporary fashion-obsessed audiences is that they have done so in a way that appears neither jaded nor calculated. Their willingness to experiment reflects a generation that consumes fashion voraciously, instinctually moving on to whatever sampler platter comes next. It takes a certain amount of bravery, after all, to associate your brand with names as far apart on a scale of fustiness as Chloë Sevigny and Hickey Freeman. And yet, at Opening Ceremony, it all still comes out looking cool. ◆

THE EARLY YEARS

Patrik Ervell photographed
by Terry Richardson, 2011.

Patrik Ervell with Carol and Humberto on 2001

Fashion designer Patrik Ervell was one of the first abiding members of the Opening Ceremony universe. He was still an editor at V Magazine *(and Humberto's roommate) when he launched his first collections at the store. Since then, Patrik's menswear has developed a loyal following for its purity and precisely cut silhouettes, and in 2011 he branched into similarly restrained womenswear collections. With his studio still located above the store, Patrik has always remained close, even as he and Opening Ceremony have grown exponentially. Carol and Humberto chatted with their fellow UC Berkeley alumnus, friend, neighbor, and colleague about the years before the store, and all that has happened since.*

PATRIK: We all went to UC Berkeley around the same time, before we moved to New York. Back then, Humberto, you were dressing and thinking about fashion in a way that your peers weren't, and it was very noticeable to me.

HUMBERTO: That's a nice way of saying I stood out!

PATRIK: I remember some Velcro fluorescent Miu Miu shoes and a backpack that looked like a jetpack. I was not necessarily on the same page, but I was definitely thinking about fashion, too. And then when you graduated you lived in San Francisco and had a weird loft. It was a converted industrial space that looked like a weird village. It was a big white open space and each person's room looked like a miniature house. It was very Humberto—it could have been an early Opening Ceremony store concept. It had the same spirit, the same point of view.

CAROL: And you knew Kate and Laura Mulleavy from Rodarte at Berkeley, too.

PATRIK: Yes, I had a few art history classes with them. Berkeley is a huge school but there was a small circle of creative people, which included the two of you and Kate and Laura.

HUMBERTO: And also Sally Singer and Patrick Li. There is this group of people that work in fashion that went to UC Berkeley. It's not a very fashionable place! Do you think that there was something about that unexpected environment that was conducive to creation?

PATRIK: It is unexpected. But I think that the San Francisco Bay Area, including Berkeley during that period, was not as peripheral of a place to be as some people say. In hindsight, it was a very culturally significant place to be. The entire culture of the Internet was being created there right at that moment. Important cultural shifts have taken place in San Francisco

and that region before anywhere else.

CAROL: That's true. I never felt that it was in any way an uninteresting or irrelevant place to be.

PATRIK: No! The first cracks in the 50s monoculture and mainstream culture happened in the Bay Area: the Free Speech Movement and the first student protest movements happened in Berkeley. 1970s counterculture, the local food movement that started with Alice Waters of Chez Panisse— these are things that changed the world. People talk about California being this weird place where things bubble up; Joan Didion writes about this all the time. People in the fashion industry think that Yves Saint Laurent putting a woman into a tuxedo is revolutionary—it's not. That's an insignificant thing compared to the cultural changes that began in California.

CAROL: That's true. I think that California teaches a creative and entrepreneurial approach to the world. But it's still kind of off the grid in terms of the fashion industry and having a certain aesthetic.

PATRIK: That's not what it specializes in, somehow; it's not about that. But I think coming from a place like that gives you the time to develop those things for yourself. Northern California isn't a place where you necessarily dress creatively.

CAROL: I can't believe I didn't know you at Berkeley! You and I didn't meet until you and Humberto were roommates one summer while you were interning at *V Magazine*. In the apartment on Walker Street that later became the Proenza Schouler office and then the Joseph Altuzarra office.

PATRIK: Yes, you came to visit and that's when I remember you guys first talking about opening a store.

HUMBERTO: Do you remember when we started the store?

PATRIK: Yes, totally. It was soon after September 11th. I was working at *V*, and after the attacks on the World Trade Center we thought the best thing was to find out who was starting up again and rebuilding, so we covered Opening Ceremony right when it opened. It was uncharted territory for a lot of people who were starting businesses at the time. No one knew what was going on or what would happen next. If you wanted to start something that was brand new or had no context, it was a good time to do it.

HUMBERTO: Yes, it was very much a rebuilding time for downtown New York.

CAROL: You were working at *V*, but you were already making things for the store.

PATRIK: I made some screen printed t-shirts. It was very basic ▸

stuff—I don't think it was even under my name. From there it was just baby steps toward creating what are now full menswear and womenswear collections. Categories were added, and it was not at all a proper business plan—everything was organic. I don't know how anyone could do that now. But that's what I did. And that's entirely because Opening Ceremony was my incubator—a safe, cozy space to develop as a designer. When the store first started, it was very much this mom and pop space, where people could try new things and experiment. There's still the spirit of that now. And I think Opening Ceremony has had that nurturing role for other brands, too.

HUMBERTO: That was definitely one of our early goals: to support our talented friends in their projects.

CAROL: Having been close to us since the beginning, how do you see the evolution of the company?

PATRIK: I remember a noticeable change, even within a few years, when the store started gaining recognition from New York establishment people—the Anna Wintours, CFDA Awards, and Barneys. They sat up and took notice; there was something notable that these people were responding to. People can feel when something is significant and relevant. And now Opening Ceremony is a benchmark for a certain designer, customer, crowd, or age group.

HUMBERTO: But we've never catered to any kind of fashion establishment. I think we've tried to stay open to a lot of scenes and creative people outside of the fashion world.

PATRIK: What makes New York a special place is the fact that these worlds mix. And Opening Ceremony is really good at bringing people together and setting up projects. This mixing of high and low, different worlds, things that don't naturally go together, the unexpected—that's the New York magic. ◈

2001 BERKELEY

THE CHEESE BOARD COLLECTIVE

WE LOVE THAT IT'S A COOP!
THE PIZZA IS TO DIE FOR!

1504 / 1512
SHATTUCK AVENUE

cheeseboard collective . coop

SLASH CLOTHING

IF YOU ARE LOOKING FOR
LEVI'S VINTAGE, THIS IS
THE PLACE.

2840 COLLEGE AVENUE
slash denim . com

LAWRENCE HALL OF SCIENCE

IF YOU ARE INTO CYCLING,
ITS A PERFECT LOCATION
TO CYCLE TO!

1 CENTENNIAL DRIVE
lawrence hall of science . org

VIKS CHAAT & MARKET

THE BEST INDIAN
STREET FOOD
& SNACKS.
PLUS THERE IS A
MARKET ATTACHED!

2390 FOURTH STREET
viks chaat corner . com

TOP DOG

EVERY DOG IS WORTH
BARKING FOR, BUT
THE SMOKED CHICKEN
APPLE DOG MAKES
US FEEL
"HEALTHY."

2534 DURANT AVENUE
top dog hotdogs . com

2002

MAKS

FOR W
WITH S
DUMPL
BEEF

77 W
STREE
CENTR

ONE

DEL

1 HAI
GRANI
WAN C
grand

BEE (

BEEF
MORE

SHOP
LANG
ARGY
MONG
bch.

LEFT: Carol, Cynthia Leung, and Humberto in Berkeley; RIGHT: Humberto's student ID card.

Berkeley has always been an enabler of dreams, a symbol of who we are and what we can become. Our students represent our best hope for California and the world. We are proud of the accomplishments of Berkeley alumni Carol Lim '97 and Humberto Leon '97, who through their company, Opening Ceremony, exemplify the best of Berkeley.

CHANCELLOR ROBERT J. BIRGENEAU, UNIVERSITY OF CALIFORNIA, BERKELEY

At Berkeley, Carol and Humberto hung out with this ripped stockinged, heavy eyelined, chain-smoking, badass crew. I remember seeing them most days as I walked on to campus, standing around looking badassy. Even then they had their own sense of style: Northern Cali goth chic—a little Morrissey meets sunshine prep.

SUCHIN PAK, JOURNALIST, "MTV NEWS," *DAILY CANDY*

Totally Killer, Awesomely Rad, and Forever Keepin' It Real: The Epic Pre-History of OC

CYNTHIA LEUNG

Before there was Opening Ceremony, there were two teenagers in early 90s suburban LA, heading to pool parties, driving to the beach, chilling at the mall, and watching *90210*. Senior proms were themed "End of the Road" after the Boyz II Men ballad. Hair was sprayed high. Humberto and Carol cruised the same highways, radios tuned in to KROQ, but had not yet met. The epic empire of Opening Ceremony is built on their soon-to-be shared myths (and labels) of suburban California, ones even more real than the slick scenes sold on *The O.C.*

Humberto was crowned high school homecoming king. Carol was voted Most Likely to Succeed. As overachieving Asian-American kids, partying was leavened with responsibility to family and work. Getting a 4.0 GPA was merely average. Humberto got held up at gunpoint scooping ice cream at Baskin Robbins. Carol preached the natural wonders of The Body Shop creams at the mall. She was often the designated driver—the one at the party who gamely kept sober to usher the drunk kids home. Humberto drove a cherry red Honda Civic with cow-print seat covers, and had a gorgeous girlfriend named Mary.

I introduced Humberto and Carol to each other in our sophomore year of college. It was the mid 90s at U.C. Berkeley, which, while proud of the excellent reputation of its liberal arts program, decidedly did not offer a major in fashion. Fashion was frowned upon, as if you were unserious, wasting your brains, SAT score, and education (and therefore, your entire life). In this embryonic, pre-Facebook, pre-cell phone, pre-blog, pre-dot-com era, if you were remotely curious about fashion, you were isolated. Naturally, you had to hunt down and befriend those whom you sensed had a similar curiosity. On this hunt, you sent little signs, some bait: a shaggy mohair cardigan, like Kurt Cobain's; a boy's haircut like Jenny Shimizu; a wife-beater like the CK ones (barely) worn by Kate Moss and Marky Mark; wooden Fleuvogs like Lady Miss Kier.

You had no way of knowing what was on the high-fashion runways until *Vogue* arrived in the mail—and when it did, the images were three months old, crushingly aspirational. So after Art History 10, we all hung out on the steps of Sproul Hall which, in the 60s, was a stage for the Free Speech Movement, and in the 90s, a public runway for fashion subcultures.

Fashion Anthropology 10: the Cholas, the insanely cool Latinas pining for Morrissey, wore one lipstick—Paramount, by MAC. The Skaters wore Dickies overalls; the Ravers wore them too, but with Fresh Jive t-shirts (secretly purchased at Hot Topic), platform sneakers, and mini backpacks à la Prada. The Mod kids raided army surplus stores for nylon bomber jackets. California kids wore The Gap and Levi's with North Face puffer jackets. Everyone sagged their jeans. It was a full-speed blender of kids from different classes, races, and tribes. Above all, it was an exhilarating freedom to explore your identity through clothes, not only through books. If, as Joan Didion wrote, "Style is character," then we had a literal right to examine that, too.

In Mass Communication 10, Humberto introduced himself by saying he liked my Doc Martens. That was enough to start a now 18-year-old friendship. In solidarity, we got matching black leather Mossimo backpacks from Nordstrom and baby-tees from Urban Outfitters. We chewed Haribo Gummi Peaches to stay awake in Political Science 10, worked in crappy restaurants together, and subsisted on the Chinese short ribs that Humberto's mom sent home in freezer bags.

At some point, maybe junior year, a kind of creative mafia crystallized at Berkeley. Armed with a landline and an absurdist sense of humor, Humberto created a pre-Facebook social network that would shame Kevin Bacon: Humberto knew Patrik Ervell, who had Art History with the Rodarte sisters, who knew Todd Selby, who knew the music-guy George Chen, who knew the art kid Mariah Robertson, who knew Humberto. And if Humberto wore Levi's Sta-Prest trousers, suddenly everyone wore Sta-Prest.

I met Carol at the Unit III dorms. Our first friend-date was at the glamorous dorm cafeteria. Carol kept it real; she was loyal and wasn't a snob. She was the glue that held everyone together and made everyone feel okay with themselves at any party. She wore jeans and J.Crew, and if you took her to the Salvation Army, she would walk out with a single cashmere sweater and promptly take it to the dry cleaners. Carol didn't hang out with the hipsters. She hung out with the brawny-brainy guys on the rugby team who were destined to get Harvard MBAs before ruling the world. And Carol was clearly on the MBA track too, but then got derailed.

Sophomore year, Carol and I moved into a tiny house with three other girls. Carol was obviously the den mother—*for sure* she was in charge of the bills—yet she set the tone of the house with her mischievous streak: it was two-to-a-room and girl hijinks galore.

It was in our sunny living room that Carol and Humberto met. It was an immediate hit, but not yet clear that they would become retailers of the decade. At the end of sophomore year, I flew to LA to visit Humberto and Carol, who were staying at their parents' houses for the summer. The three of us went for a night out at The Viper Room, where we shyly spied Kate Moss and Johnny Depp embracing in a nearly empty club. Kate was wearing a 1950s tulle crinoline. Johnny was post-*21 Jump Street* and pre-*Pirates*; River Phoenix was still alive. It was the precise touch of glamour that we were all yearning for.

Although we giddily drank in this awesome celeb-glam cocktail, to be honest, I think we were all crazier about our one hour of getting ready together at Humberto's mom's house, when we pieced together our going out ensembles with Saint Etienne on the CD player. We were playing grown-up, with no other care except to idealize a fashion utopia torn from the pages of a magazine. It was California dreaming. But eventually, Opening Ceremony realized it. ◆

Good Thing He Didn't Listen to Me

Spike Jonze talks to Humberto's mom, Wendy Leon… & Carol's family!

Spike Jonze and Wendy Leon
at the opening of Opening
Ceremony at the Ace Hotel,
2010. Cover of *Good Thing
He Didn't Listen to Me*, Spike
Jonze, published by Opening
Ceremony Press, 2012:
Original artwork by Marcel
Dzama, courtesy Marcel
Dzama and David Zwirner,
New York: "Strange Birds",
2006, Ink and gouache on
paper, 14 x 11".

Opening Ceremony. Who would name a store that? It's like naming your son "Running Down the Street Wolinski." It's just weird, you know what I mean? I remember when I first heard of the store and its name, I thought a lot about what an abstract name it was. It was one of those things where I didn't understand it and I was impressed by it, and the combination of those two things freaked me out. And the store itself was hard to pin down. It was obviously something special and unique. And it didn't have anything to do with what other stores were doing, but you could tell it was made by a person or a group of people that were making something they were excited about.

About five years ago I met the founders of Opening Ceremony, Carol Lim and Humberto Leon, and it started making more sense. They weren't fashion people—they were normal people. They'd been friends for years and they'd started this thing out of a love for people doing creative things—travel, eating good food, and maybe most of all, creating a place that would bring all their friends together. I've been lucky enough to be let into this circle of them and their friends. It's hard to explain Carol and Humberto and why they're so special but hopefully by the time you read this introduction you'll get a sense of why I love them so much.

When I met Humberto's mom, who had immigrated from China to LA when Humberto was born, it made even more sense. Wendy Leon is an important part of the OC universe: she often travels the world with Carol, Humberto, and Carol's mom, Heidi, and cooks big meals for staff and friends wherever she is. She's endlessly positive and fearless and strong-willed, which is how I'd describe Humberto and Carol and the company they've built.

SPIKE JONZE

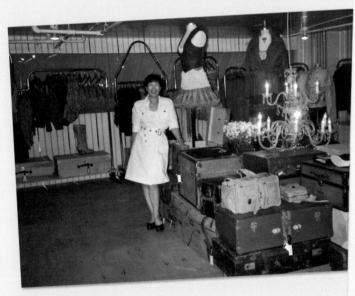

CLOCKWISE FROM TOP LEFT:
Wendy in Hong Kong, age 17;
age 12; age 12; Wendy at the
New York store, 2003.

SPIKE: Wendy, can you tell me a little bit about where you're from?

WENDY: I'm from China, but in 1956, when I was nine, I went to Hong Kong. I worked with my grandma as a little maid. I was living in somebody else's house. My grandma was in charge of the whole house, but I had to do all of the cleaning. At that time, they paid me $50 a month.

Can you tell me about when you left your family?

My family was in China, and my grandma always came over to see us once a year. My mom said, "Hey, come here. You want to go with grandma and go on the boot-boot chair?" They don't call it "bus" in my country, they call it "boot-boot chair," because the bus, the horn is *boot, boot, boot*. I was so excited, we had never seen a bus until my grandma was leaving, and we were taking her to the bus stop when we saw the big, huge bus. My mom gave me a nice outfit and gave me new shoes. She said, "Go with your grandma. My cousin, she is your godmother. She doesn't have any daughters, so she wants you to go there and be there with her." I was like, "Yeah! Why not?"

The next day was exciting, I was dressed up nice and had combed hair, and then my dad had a bicycle, so he took me, my grandma, my mom, my brother, and my sister, and we all went far away. It was like an hour bike ride to go there. I was so happy. I had the biggest smile. I was so excited to go in the bus, jumping around, and people kept coming in. Then my bus finally moved…. Something wasn't right.

I climbed to the window where my family still lined the roadside watching the bus. They all stood there somberly, staring at me with expressions that I couldn't understand. It was then that I noticed my mother's face was wet. Tears. I started to pound the window with an open palm. The bus was pulling away. I watched in confusion as my father grabbed his bicycle and started to ride after the bus, as if he'd changed his mind and was going to stop the vehicle. He rode after us for awhile and then stopped. The tears started to well up as what was happening began to dawn on me for the first time.

I realized that I don't have my family anymore, I'm only with grandma. I couldn't stop crying. My grandma kept on telling me, "You cannot cry because your family needs you, you're the one. Your godmother chose you. You're lucky she didn't choose your sister, because she thinks you're more smart and that's why she chose you. Your family needs you. If you don't support your family, they're done." I just cried. Nonstop crying for four, five hours on a bus. By the time I went to the immigration in China, I told myself, I said, "Okay, I think I won't let you down. Whatever you want me to do, I'll do it for you. I promise. I need to take care of you guys." I promised myself.

And what did you do? What was your job?

I cleaned the house and served the food for the rich people, the family. I cleaned clothes, ironed—everything my grandmother wanted me to do, but she checked me really hard. She made sure they didn't fire me.

When did you begin work on a normal day?

Six o'clock in the morning until midnight, sleeping time, or until we were done. But sometimes I was tired, and in the afternoon my grandma let me take a half-hour nap when nobody was home. At first I cried a lot. I missed my family. But my grandma kept on telling me, "Your family needs you."

And how long did you work there?

I worked as a maid for three or four years. And then later on, the next door [neighbors] knew I was working so hard and doing a good job, so they wanted to pay more. They told my grandma, "I want her to come to my house." But I couldn't go with my grandma, I had to go by myself. With my grandma I was getting paid $50 a month, but at the new house, I would get paid $100 a month. A lot of money to my grandma. She was thinking, "Before, every two months I sent $100 to China," but now she said, "You can send $100 every month!" That's why she moved me to another house.

Now you're not the little maid, you're the big maid.

Still a little maid, but [I had to work] harder. Not like my grandma would cover for me, you know? I did everything on my own. She told me, "You have to do that, do that, do that, do that…and then if you turn around and you don't finish it, they'll yell at you."

The amazing thing about Wendy is that when she tells her story, most of the time she's laughing, and all of the time ▶

she's smiling, even when there are tears rolling down her face.

Through her teenage years, Wendy continued working in Hong Kong, cooking and cleaning seven days a week, from 6 am until midnight every day, always sending money back home. Eventually she got married and had two kids. Her husband, Ricardo, spent much of his time out of town, so she didn't see him that often. One day Ricardo and her mother-in-law showed up at the house and took her out for dim sum to tell her something.

Something was wrong, and I knew it. I was terrified of what was coming. She said, "Well aren't you going to eat?" "No, I'm nervous. What do you want to talk about?" My mother-in-law sighed and put down her chopsticks. She looked over at Ricardo. "Papa Ricardo is afraid to tell you something." She looked at her son again. I turned to Ricardo, sitting there, silent as stone. "Actually, he has one daughter." I was rooted to my chair, frozen, as if time had stopped. "She's from another woman, way before Ricardo met you." I cried when I got home, upset because I never knew, upset because Ricardo never told me, upset because I somehow felt responsible for this child but could barely feed [my daughter] and myself.

One year later, her mother-in-law came to visit her again, and told her that Ricardo actually had two more children from yet another relationship. The church where the children had been staying was closing, and they needed a place to live, so Wendy took them in. With a full house, working seven days a week, she found out she was pregnant with another child.

I hoped to lose it. I lived on the sixth floor, and I never took the elevator, I always walked the six floors, hoping the baby comes out. I would keep jumping and jumping [to try to lose it].

One day I fell, and I was knocked out in the bathroom because I think the medicine I was taking was too strong. I had a roommate—she picked me up and gave me oil. She said, "Don't do that, it's your kid, it's your kid. Keep it, God doesn't want you to do that." So I kept the baby, and that baby was Humberto.

My mother-in-law said "You should have your baby born in America. At least when he's 18 years old, he can bring you guys back to the US. He'll be an American citizen."

So you snuck in to America to have your baby?

Yes, seven months [pregnant]. It's wintertime, it's really cold. I have a heavy jacket and two kids. They kept me busy in immigration, but they didn't see that I was pregnant because I wore so many clothes.

Once Wendy got to the US, she began working in a garment factory in downtown Los Angeles. One day she was going into labor. So she walked a few miles to the hospital, having to stop every few blocks to sit down due to the pain. She finally made it to the hospital and Humberto, a nine-pound baby, was born.

How would you describe Humberto as a child?

When he was a child, he was a really good kid. I worked at a restaurant. I had to bring him and carry him Chinese style, cooking in a fast food place, wearing him on my back. When he was sleeping—they had a big bag of rice, 100 pounds—I put him on top of the rice to sleep, and he slept for a couple of hours.

I also worked sewing clothes. I brought home clothes every day. I had to make 100 [pieces]—one dollar a piece. If I didn't pass $100, I wouldn't stop [until] 3:00, 4:00 in the morning.

And you worked at the restaurant during the day?

Yeah.

So a few years later, you opened a restaurant, right?

Yes, by that time, I had brought a lot more of my family here. Eight of my brothers and sisters came over, and they all worked in the restaurant business, but in the kitchen. So I opened a small restaurant for them all to work at, in Crenshaw, in downtown Los Angeles. It was called Dynasty Garden. Humberto was the only one in the restaurant that spoke English, so he translated the to-go orders.

How old was he?

Oh, when he was ten years old he already worked as a busboy, cashier, took to-go orders, answered the phones, ▸

CLOCKWISE FROM TOP
LEFT: Humberto at age 8;
Humberto's birthday at
McDonald's, age 4; School
photo, age 11; Huntington
Beach, California, age 13.

and translated for my brother. Later on, when we were getting successful, we opened a bigger restaurant—200 seats in Arcadia. Humberto always worked full time with me. Friday nights, Saturday, and Sunday. He never went anywhere. Never took a day off or had play dates with his friends. He was working the whole time. My two daughters worked in the morning as busboys, serving some food, but my son always stayed to the end.

In high school, he had a few different jobs at the mall. He always loved the mall. He worked squeezing lemonade and he worked for 31 Ice Cream (Baskin Robbins). That's why he got all the ice cream free—all he could eat. But he was interested in working for the Gap. He ended up working there part time, 20 hours a week. Then he moved to Berkeley for college. He still worked for Gap as part time.

Did you get the sense that he always liked clothes? Was he always interested in fashion?

Yeah, I think, yes. Because, I'll show you. [*She pulls out a photograph*] His first project he did for Berkeley. I went to see him and I said, "Oh my goodness, what are you doing?" I had to take him to my friend's factory to buy the material: 100 yards of white material. I said, "What are you doing?" He said, "I'm doing a bra." I said, "What bra? A woman's bra? Why do you need 100 yards?" He said, "Mom, you don't understand."

It was a giant woman's bra?

Giant, 100 yards.

When you saw it, did you understand that it was a creative project?

I didn't, I didn't. No.

What did he dress like in college?

Sometimes he dressed up old-fashioned, but you cannot tell it's old-fashioned to us. To us, it looks like new fashion. But I said, "Oh, I think I was nine, ten years old. I've seen that before in my times."

He always dressed like that?

He dressed up different, he wore white shirts. The first time Carol's mom met Humberto, he was wearing a white shirt, like a high school white shirt and tight black pants.

He was wearing a bow tie. Carol's mom said, "Why is this little boy dressed up like that? I don't like it." Carol said, "Mom, don't say that! He's really smart. Maybe some day he'll be somebody, don't say that! This is his style." "Oh really? I'm not really impressed." Even Carol's mom told me that: It's so funny.

At Berkeley, Humberto met Carol, who would become his closest friend and partner over the next 20 years. I think their relationship is at the heart of what makes Opening Ceremony work and so special. They're real partners in every way—they live in the same apartment building, they go on vacations together, they hang out with the same group of friends, they take care of each other when they're sick. They're partners in life together, in every way, except romantically. Probably because they both like guys.

What do you think made Humberto and Carol's friendship so special?

Carol smiles a lot. She's a really honest person. And fun! Her and Humberto have the same attitude. They talk the same. Same friends, same jokes. They love food and travel. She is very polite. She respects older people—that is the most important thing, you know. [*laughs*] And that's why I think she is close to Humberto like that. He is like that, too. I consider Carol my daughter and Humberto and her are like brother and sister. They do things together, they care for each other. They're like a family—we're like a family. Me and her parents are like a family.

After college, Humberto continued working at the Gap and eventually designed the Old Navy stores for them when they started that chain. He got so much attention that he was hired away by Burberry to redesign all of their stores. So, at 25 years old, he moved to New York. Carol was working in San Francisco as an investment planner and then also moved to New York six months later to work at Bally as a merchandising planner.

What did Humberto do for Burberry?

He was in charge of redesigning all of the stores at Burberry. I was so proud. He invited me to the opening of the first store. They all told me how proud they were ▸

CLOCKWISE FROM TOP LEFT:
Humberto, age 6; in Hong
Kong, 1982; playing tennis,
age 11; in Berkeley, age 20.
FOLLOWING PAGE, CLOCKWISE
FROM TOP LEFT: Carol and
Humberto, Berkeley, both
age 20; Humberto's college
art project, Berkeley, 1995;
Humberto's first year at
Berkeley, age 18.

of my son. Everybody lined up to talk to me and say how impressed they were, and that they could not work without him. But one day at lunch, he said, "Mom, I want to open a business in New York." I was shocked because I thought he had such a good job and so much power.

I said, "But I don't feel comfortable that you'd open up a business." I didn't have enough money to support him if something went wrong. He said, "Don't worry about it, we'll figure it out." But I was worried. Opening a business is not easy, and they were so young. And he had a good job and a good title. I was scared, but he wouldn't listen. He said, "Mom, don't worry. If we open a business and it fails and doesn't work out, I can always go back to my job. But at least I tried." It's a good thing he didn't listen to me.

Are you happy that Carol is in New York looking out for Humberto because you aren't here to take care of him?

Oh, I always thank her. I cry. Every single time I see her, I say, "Carol, thank you for being there for Humberto

today." I thank her for making everything happen with Humberto. Every single time I tell her thank you. She always cries and hugs me.

Do you worry about Humberto less because Carol is there?

When Humberto and Carol are together, I am not worried at all. I know they take care of each other. Even when Carol had surgery, I called him and I said, "Are you taking care of her?" And he said, "Of course mom, I am the first person to be next to her." And Humberto gets a really bad headache once in a while, once a year, and Carol knows how to take care of him. She says, "Go in your room, shut off all the lights and sleep for a half hour."

So Carol knows how to take care of him?

Sometimes he forgets to rest, and will continue to work. And Carol will say, "No, no, no, remember you have to go lay down for a half hour and then you'll be okay."

So in the fall of 2002, Humberto and Carol started Opening Ceremony. They got a small retail space on Howard Street, which at the time was in an unfashionable part of SoHo. It had been a Chinese massage parlor before, so rent wasn't that expensive. They were the only employees. They wanted the store to carry clothes and things made by young creative people from all over the world. To find young designers and artists that weren't known outside of their countries. Every year they would focus the store on a different country. They saw themselves as an international melting pot. So they named themselves Opening Ceremony, based on the opening ceremonies of the Olympic games. When I learned what it meant, the name seemed less abstract, but equally inspired.

What did you remember about Carol and Humberto starting the store?

I asked them, "Where will you get the clothes?" He said, "Mom, the first thing I want to sell are clothes from Hong Kong. Can you go with us to Hong Kong and buy stuff?" So I went with him and Carol. We went to a little hotel. It was so expensive—$150 a day. We would go shopping all day and then pack it into plastic bags all night. We had to roll the clothes into tight, little bundles so we could pack more into our suitcases.

So he was finding all these designers in Hong Kong that had never sold outside of Hong Kong.

Yeah, no, never.

They brought all their money with them?

We used a lot of credit cards. And they'd gotten a loan from a bank. We bought as many clothes as we could fit in the luggage we brought. We each had two giant bags that by the time they were stuffed with these rolled up clothes, they were too heavy for us to even lift.

So you had them in your suitcases so you could get them through customs without declaring them?

Yeah in our suitcases and bags. Then, when we got to New York, we would iron everything and if it was broken we had to sew it and fix it. And we hung everything in the store, but then no people came in. I was very nervous.

How long was it before people started coming in?

I think it was a month. And then they started wandering in and buying the clothes from Hong Kong. And then it was buy, buy, buy. And then we were worried that there wasn't enough clothes, because the first batch had sold out so quickly. That's why we had to take another trip back to Hong Kong so soon. We brought more people this time. You can only bring two pieces of luggage per person, so we had to bring more people to buy more clothes. Carol and Humberto brought their friends, and they brought all the money they'd made from the first batch. And we brought those clothes back and they sold out even quicker.

Humberto said in that first year, that they had to do 14 trips back to Hong Kong.

Yeah, many trips, rolling and rolling clothes into little bundles, as many as we could get into the bags.

The funny thing about Humberto and Carol is both of them are so low key that when they started the store neither of them actually wanted to sell anything to customers. They were both too embarrassed, because they didn't want anyone to feel like they were pushing anything on them. So they would sit in the back and watch customers through a peephole, and if somebody wanted to buy something they would laugh and fight about who had to go out and help them.

Yeah, they wanted to give them the freedom. Even now, he does it. That's his style, I think. Because he hates people following him when he's at other stores. He's looking at something and people are following him around, trying to sell the merchandise, like "Oh, do you need help?" pressuring him. He hates that. That's why he doesn't want to do that to people. That's why he kept a little peephole.

What does he tell employees as far as when people come to the store?

He wants the employees to give the customers a lot of freedom. Don't force them to buy and don't force them to try. Sometimes they have a movie star come in. You cannot stare at them, you cannot take pictures with them—you have to leave them alone. I think they are really smart. I learned ▶

so much from Carol and Humberto. I saw the way they did it—it's really professional. Also, I think they are good bosses, they have good hearts. They want something, they're really strict. They won't say, "Oh, because you're my friend you can do whatever you want." No. He's really strict but afterward, he still is your good friend. I think they have good hearts. And together, they have magic brains.

Magic brains?

Yeah. They know each other so well. You know, she knows exactly what he's thinking and he knows exactly what she's thinking.

What does Carol bring to the business that makes it what it is?

They do everything together. He cannot work without Carol. Even when I'm at home with him, I'll ask him something about OC, and he'll say, "I don't know, I have to ask Carol." He'll never give you a straight answer—he has to ask Carol. And her, too. Every single time people ask her something, she responds the same way, "Oh, I have to ask Humberto."

In the first year, they hired Olivia, who was their first employee, and it was just the three of them in that one store.

When did you stop being worried?

As soon as he came back from Hong Kong, and I saw all the people buying the clothes, I wasn't worried anymore. I would go to New York and visit him and all the customers would tell me how great he is and how good he is. They all came to talk to me, and everybody would tell me, so I knew they were successful.

Over the years, the store grew, and the company became more successful, and they had to hire more and more people, but they always tried to maintain the heart of it. Humberto once told me a story about how after they'd had the store for a few years, a few of their friends had gone in and the employees had given them attitude. At first Humberto didn't believe it, because he liked everyone that worked there. But after enough people told him that, he realized it was true and that something had changed. Some of the people that worked there had started developing an attitude that they were cool, and they started treating customers poorly. Humberto and Carol called a meeting with

all the employees after hours, and they talked about what the store meant to them, and when Humberto started talking about how upset he was, that it had turned into this other thing and that he'd heard how people were being treated, he started to cry because he was so disappointed. And then Carol started to cry, and then everyone started to cry. And everyone understood what it meant to Humberto and Carol and everyone either changed or eventually weeded themselves out and left the company.

So now, ten years later, Opening Ceremony has five stores in LA, New York, and Tokyo. All of the most interesting companies in the world come to them to do collaborations; they design their own line; they have an online store and blog. Humberto and Carol are now the creative directors of Kenzo, a big French fashion line. And Opening Ceremony continues in the spirit in which they started it.

Can you think of a moment when you've been with them where they've been the most excited in the last ten years?

Of course when they open a store, we are all very excited. On my 60th birthday we went to Japan on a vacation. We went with Carol's mom, too. They had a meeting with a person in Japan, and they came home really late. And Carol was drunk that night in Japan. And they were both very happy. And Humberto told me, "Mom, we might be opening a store next year in Japan because we met the person." And it happened so fast. And the next year we all came back to open the store. We all went there. And it was so much fun. All of our family came and all of Carol's family came, and they opened a big store in the middle of Tokyo that was eight stories tall. I was so happy and so excited and so proud. On the opening day, as I watched them, I started crying, and I couldn't stop. I watched them during this big opening celebration, and it made me so happy. I was thinking about when I was nine years old and I was a little maid, and now I have become this woman getting to watch my son...and I was a really poor person with no education or anything. Today, my son brings me everywhere like I'm somebody. In Tokyo, I was so happy and crying—not like sad crying, you know? And all of their friends were there. I'm so proud of him. Of both of them.

임선 Carol

humberto.

If you had to explain it to me, what is Opening Ceremony?

Opening Ceremony is like—the name is so powerful. You have a celebration. Every day, people walk in to the store and feel like Opening Ceremony. Everything is fresh, you feel the name, you feel the store. But it's more than a store. It can be anything. It could be a bar one day, a movie, anything. Humberto and Carol, they love to eat. They love food. They are never ending. Their brains are thinking of one thing only—of what excites them. Maybe someday you'll see, "Oh, Opening Ceremony has a market, a store, a restaurant." They always surprise me. They love to travel, they love to eat, they love their friends, they love to have a party. And all of that is in Opening Ceremony. They enjoy every single minute. They have so much energy and are always thinking of new things. That's what Opening Ceremony is. Opening Ceremony is never ending. Every day it's a surprise. ◆

LEFT: Carol and Humberto, photographed by Sebastian Kim, 2009; RIGHT: in Berkeley, age 19.

CLOCKWISE FROM TOP LEFT:
Carol, Northridge, CA, age 12;
age 7; Carol in Hawaii, 2004;
school photo, age 5. Back cover
of *Good Thing He Didn't Listen
to Me*, Spike Jonze, published
by Opening Ceremony Press,
2012: Original artwork by
Marcel Dzama, courtesy
Marcel Dzama and David
Zwirner, New York: "The Class
of 2002," 2011, Ink and
gouache on paper, 14 x 11″.

When Carol Had a Snoopy Suitcase

Spike Jonze continues his biographical piece on Carol and Humberto by interviewing Carol's mom, Heidi Lim, and her brother, Albert Lim.

SPIKE: Tell me what Carol was like as a little girl.

HEIDI: When she was in preschool, I went in for a parent-teacher conference, and the teacher told me Carol was like the den mother because she would always tell people what to do. The teacher said, "Carol is great, but if there's an assignment, she'll go around showing other people how to do their work before she even finishes it herself."

No way!

ALBERT: Oh yeah, she was like this very early on.

So she was both bossy and she took care of everybody?

ALBERT: She was actually really bratty as a kid. We got in a lot of fights!

HEIDI: Yes, I told Carol once: "If you fight with your brother one more time, I'm going to send you to the orphanage." And when she was naughty again, I pretended to call the orphanage and said, "Hello, I am bringing my daughter to you." So I packed up Carol's Snoopy suitcase and took her to the car.

ALBERT: At that point Carol was in tears, screaming, "All right! I'll do whatever you say!"

And when did she stop being a brat and become the Carol we know and love?

HEIDI: In high school, she started thinking about the family and other people. She wanted to work herself.

ALBERT: Her first job was at The Body Shop, and because it was green-oriented she turned vegetarian and started getting into Save the Earth movements. She organized things at school and got really into the environment.

How does the family relate with Carol now that she's the head of this super successful business?

ALBERT: We're at the point where I go to her for advice on stuff, even though I'm the older brother. She's always the problem solver. Before the due date for a project, a show, or opening, it all seems to come together, and we just kind of have faith in that. On family vacations she always deals with everything.

And you were saying that sometimes your family just takes it for granted, because everyone just knows that Carol's going to make it all happen?

ALBERT: She needs to hear it from us, too—that she's amazing, that she's done an amazing job. It's something we never tell her. I don't know why. You know, my dad is a very stoic Asian man, so that's not his style. So it really has to come from me and my mom.

It's kind of jaw-dropping how much Opening Ceremony has developed, and how much she's done. Just thinking back on the early days in 2002, there would be days when people just wouldn't walk in [the store]. It was really through her stewardship that this whole thing blossomed into what it is. It's just mind-blowing.

HEIDI: I watch her and I think, "How can you do that? You're so incredible." ◆

⊸ The class of 2002 ⟿

Francis   Olivia   SU   Carol

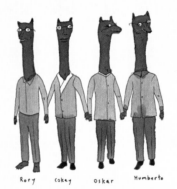

Rory   cokey   Oskar   Humberto

Bettina   Jayne   Jenny   Jacky   Nicole   Vamberto

Frosty   Shirley   Jesse   marcel dzama

opening
ceremony
press

2002

HONG KONG

Lazaro Hernandez and Jack
McCollough photographed
by Terry Richardson, 2011.

Jack McCollough and Lazaro Hernandez with Carol and Humberto on 2002

Jack McCollough and Lazaro Hernandez of New York fashion brand Proenza Schouler launched their first collection the same year that Carol and Humberto established Opening Ceremony. But their friendship was founded a few years earlier when, by chance, Humberto cast the young Parsons students for a Dior Homme campaign. Fast forward a few years and Proenza's iconic PS1 bags and runway collections now sell out at our stores. The old friends sat down over drinks at the Crosby Street Hotel to talk about the past ten years in their respective businesses, both of which have become synonymous with a new, internationally recognized generation of New York fashion.

HUMBERTO: We've known you guys for ten years. We started our businesses the same year, in 2002.

CAROL: You should do something for your anniversary! When is it?

LAZARO: This September. We're not very good at celebrating our anniversaries.

HUMBERTO: We've always had a lot of mutual friends. One of the first encounters was casting you guys for the Dior campaign. I took your Polaroids in 2001. It was your last semester at Parsons. I casted 300 people for that, including Dan Colen, Brian Phillips, and Nate Lowman.

LAZARO: I remember that!

HUMBERTO: When was the first time you guys came by our store?

JACK: It was right when you opened. The first time we came, you ran down the street after a shoplifter. What did you do when you got to him?

HUMBERTO: I jumped on top of him and pinned him down. We didn't realize people would steal, as crazy as that sounds.

CAROL: It was the first time we were in retail. A lot of the interactions were new to us.

LAZARO: I feel like Opening Ceremony has always just sort of been there. As far back as I can remember, it's been a presence in my life.

JACK: It's such a New York staple. That's why I was so surprised when you said you opened in 2002. We associated it with being always around.

LAZARO: I never felt like Opening Ceremony was "up and coming" as a store.

JACK: There wasn't a slow buildup.

HUMBERTO: A lot of it had to do with the fact that we couldn't afford to buy a lot of merchandise for the store, so everything sold out really quickly. It made every item in the store seem precious.

LAZARO: In 2002, when we both started our companies, didn't you guys feel like anything was possible?

HUMBERTO: Yes, it felt like we had nothing to lose.

LAZARO: It was a convergence of things: our age, having just graduated college, having nothing. So like, what *are* you gonna lose?

JACK: It was similar for both of us, actually. When we started, the establishment brands—the Donna Karans and the Calvin Kleins—became the mass brands. And then the young guys—Marc Jacobs, Narciso Rodriguez, Michael Kors—became the establishment. And the same thing in retail: Barneys became a mass thing, Jeffrey became the establishment, and people were waiting for the next thing.

LAZARO: There was a youth culture that wasn't being addressed. A lot of our friends had taken risks and put themselves out there.

HUMBERTO: It's true. It's harder to find young designers now with the same quality and freethinking. I don't know what it is. The Internet has something to do it. We're the last generation of people who grew up without the Internet, where you actually had to dig for culture. For music, you had to go to actual music stores.

CAROL: You had to wait for your monthly subscriptions to come, and you'd read your magazines cover to cover.

LAZARO: But nowadays there's so much information.

HUMBERTO: It's really dispersed.

LAZARO: Do you guys feel old? I feel like an adult. I feel older. I feel wiser. Not as naïve. I think our naïveté served us well at the beginning. We had no fear. I feel like now, we're more cautious about the moves we have to make. I guess there's just more to lose now, to risk what you have.

HUMBERTO: I feel like I just get more involved.

JACK: Do you guys have a trajectory of what your path is going to be like in the future? Do you imagine doing this when you're 70?

HUMBERTO: I've always felt like we built our business so we can do other things. We love food, so we'd like to do a restaurant at some point.

CAROL: Retail in general is so broad. It's an experience. You go to a grocery store, you go to a clothing store, you go to ▶

a plant store. Invariably as a human being, your tastes change. As you change as a person, how do you evolve? Fashion is what we do, but our lives are so much more than that. Which is why I think the store stays relevant. We bring in everything we do proudly. It's more than thinking of clothes 24/7—it's about including traveling, food, art. It's inclusive.

LAZARO: Most of our ideas come from outside of fashion, from travel, food, movies, or music. You take from that and you make fashion. You don't take from fashion because it already exists. Our brand has always been about purity, so the minute when we're not feeling it anymore, we'll stop, that's it.

HUMBERTO: When you stop doing this, what will you be doing?

JACK: I can imagine switching it up in my 40s. I want to be able to make things on a slower level. What we do is so extroverted. It's great and we're always communicating with other people, but it would be nice to be in your head and be in a shop and design things, to use our hands in a different way.

CAROL: In our case, it's a model that keeps renewing itself. When we started [buying for] OC in 2001, we went to Hong Kong and it was all about discovering their shopping culture. Argentina, which we featured in 2011, is a great example; you find people making things with their hands when you travel around there.

HUMBERTO: When we started, we were known for bringing in weird foreign brands into the market. I feel like we want to do more of that. ◈

2002 HONG KONG

MAKS NOODLE
FOR WONTON NOODLES WITH SHRIMP DUMPLINGS AND BEEF BRISKET.
77 WELLINGTON STREET, CENTRAL

ONE HARBOUR ROAD
DELICIOUS DIM SUM!
1 HARBOUR ROAD, GRAND HYATT, WAN CHAI
grandhyatthongkong.hk

BEE CHENG HIANG
BEEF JERKY...NEED I SAY MORE?
SHOP 36, B2/F, LANGHAM PLACE, 8 ARGYLE ST, MONG KOK
bch.com.sg

RISE COMMERCIAL BUILDING
A MINI MALL WITH YOUNG DESIGNERS & SOUVENIRS
5-11 GRANVILLE CIRCUIT, KOWLOON

TSUI WAH RESTAURANT
OUR LATE NIGHT SPOT. OUR GUILTY PLEASURE: CHEESE-BAKED RICE WITH CRISPY PORK CHOPS.
15-19 WELLINGTON STREET, CENTRAL
tsuiwahrestaurant.com

OCEAN EMPIRE FOOD SHOP
OUR FAVORITE QUICK BREAKFAST SPOT
NO 4-5 ON G/F., EXCELSIOR PLAZA, 24-26 EAST POINT ROAD, CAUSEWAY BAY

2003

RITZ
YOU'LL
INTO S
KNOW
NEIGHB
RESTA
ALAME
JARDI

CLUBE
SUPER
RVA F
BELA
aloca

STILL
DANCE
AWAY
AVENI
DE M
BARR
d-edg

Hong Kong Market, 2002. LEFT PAGE: Sai Kung Beach, 2002.

We found a home for Opening Ceremony on Howard Street at the edge of SoHo!

When Carol and Humberto brought Opening Ceremony to a little-traveled block of Howard Street, the neighborhood was an unexpected haven straddling Chinatown and SoHo. Previously, 35 Howard Street had been a linen store above a basement massage parlor. In those early days, rats and trash were more common than shoppers, an ironic past for a cross street that is now a fashion destination, home to Jil Sander, Derek Lam, and the Mondrian Hotel.

The original flagship store now extends onto four floors, and the Opening Ceremony empire now stretches down the street, with a shop at 33 Howard and offices on both Howard and nearby Centre Street, as well as the full archive collections, and an Opening Ceremony-operated Acne store on Greene Street.

Opening Ceremony was a pioneer in this neighborhood, as they have been with fashion retail in general.

CECILIA DEAN, *VISIONAIRE*

In 2002, Opening Ceremony's flagship store planted itself on the corner of Howard Street and Crosby Street in SoHo, two streets that are so spindly and worn and so buckling with cobblestones that they are, more accurately, aggrandized alleys.

I happened to grow up on the northern end of Crosby Street, not exactly a stone's throw, but possibly a kick-ball's kick away. Back then, SoHo had been recently settled by a community of artists, who used the vast, abandoned factory spaces and expansive windows to hoist their canvases, slosh their paint, and sell their efforts. As seductive as this nostalgia is—and as hellish as the Broadway and Prince intersection can be on a Saturday afternoon—I also remember the relative barrenness and slight loneliness of the place in the early 80s.

Now, nearly thirty years later, the artists have largely drifted out of SoHo and into the boroughs and beyond. The paintings hang on the walls of those who bought them, rather than those who made them. But there are still remnants of the past, and there is still Opening Ceremony. And now, I have had the wild fortune of befriending its two founders Humberto Leon and Carol Lim, two people whose tastes and discernments are irrefutable, but whose curiosity and enthusiasm are even more responsible for creating a store as inclusive, interactive, and fun as Opening Ceremony. Because Opening Ceremony is more than a store: it's a culture. A brilliant pop culture. And what good is cool if it isn't fun?

CLAIRE DANES, ACTOR

35 Howard Street pre-Opening Ceremony. RIGHT: Maps for Opening Ceremony New York stores, 2006-2012.

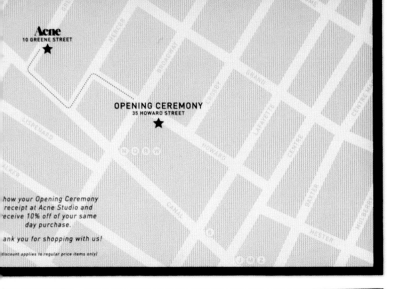

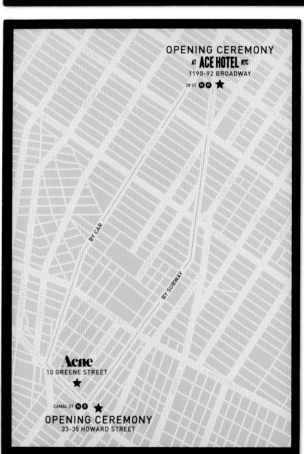

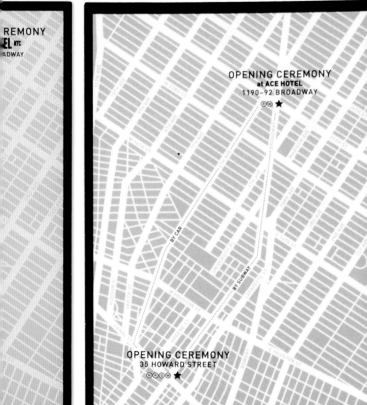

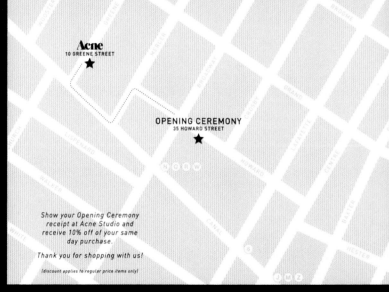

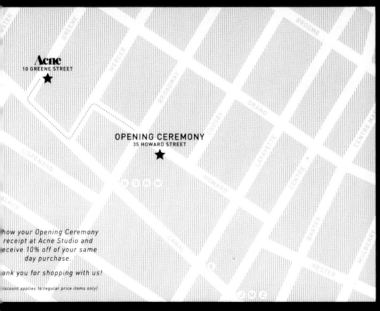

Our friends worked with us around the clock to prepare for our grand opening ceremony!

In addition to going on several buying trips to Hong Kong, Carol and Humberto spent the summer of 2002 working to get their new Howard Street space ready for its September grand opening. Using a truly DIY ethos that would become a hallmark of Opening Ceremony, they invited their friends to help out with painting, decorating, and transforming the raw space into a fully appointed boutique. For the opening party, Carol and Humberto's families guarded the merchandise, as downtown kids spilled beer on the floors and tagged the walls. Carol's godbrother, Daniel, filmed the party in nightvision, and the Super-8 film pulses with the feeling that something special has started. Over the years, the OCNY Howard Street store would grow in size and scope, while still remaining the heart and soul of the company.

You are invited to the opening of
Opening Ceremony
September 19, 2002
10pm-2am

r.s.v.p. purple@openingceremony.us

This invitation admits guest plus one

CAMPARI

Opening Ceremony
est.2002

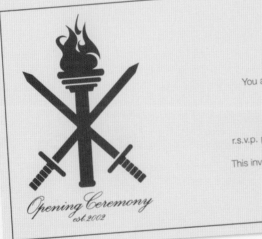

CLOCKWISE FROM TOP:
The completed store, 2002;
Stills from the opening
party, filmed by Daniel Lew;
Invitation to the opening
party. **LEFT PAGE, CLOCKWISE
FROM TOP LEFT:** Carol and
Humberto photographed
by Eric McNatt for *Paper*
magazine, November 2002;
The construction of Opening
Ceremony. **FOLLOWING
TWO SPREADS:** Opening
Ceremony New York,
2009–2012, photographed
by Michael Vahrenwald.

Opening Ceremony is one of the places that has made downtown New York the exciting destination it has become in the last ten years.

ROSEMARIE BRAVO, FORMER CEO OF BURBERRY GROUP

SHE'S WALKING DOWN THE STREET

BLIND TO EVERY ☠ SHE MEETS

DO YOU THINK YOU'LL BE THE GUY

HELLO, I LOVE YOU ♥

WON'T YOU TELL ME YOUR NAME?
hello, I love you, let me jump in your game

hello. I love you

WON'T YOU TELL ME YOUR NAME?

HELLO, I LOVE YOU, LET ME JUMP IN YOUR GAME

SHE HOLDS HER HEAD SO HIGH

LIKE A STATUE IN THE ☁ SKY

HER ARMS ARE WICKED, AND HER LEGS ARE LONG
WHEN SHE MOVES MY BRAIN SCREAMS OUT THIS SONG

— SIDEWALK CROUCHES AT HER FEET —
LIKE A DOG 🐕 THAT BEGS FOR SOMETHING SWEET

DO YOU HOPE TO MAKE HER SEE, YOU FOOL
DO YOU HOPE TO PLUCK THIS DUSKY 💎 JEWEL?

HELLO, HELLO, HELLO, HELLO
Hello, hello, hello, I want you • Hello I need my baby

HELLO, HELLO, HELLO, HELLO
hello, hello, hello

& Carol OPENING CEREMONY

Downtown New York was a pretty gloomy place in 2002. V Magazine, where I worked at the time, shot a group portrait of the Opening Ceremony team, complete with decorative red Chinese dragons, on the steps inside their store. The photograph looked like a mix between a family portrait and a co-ed intramural softball team, but it exuded a confidence, a coolness, and a bit of theatricality, all of which became the staple crops of Opening Ceremony. Companies always want to give off the impression that they're one big family, and usually that is never the truth. But Opening Ceremony really is a family. To find a successful enterprise built by two individuals who respect their employees, their customers, and even just the young folks drifting around looking for something to hear, watch, wear, try on, flip through, talk about, or drink.... It's to their credit that Opening Ceremony is a Manhattan institution that actually feels like it's only just begun, because the newness and the enthusiasm hasn't worn off at the elbows. I bought a Patrik Ervell shirt in the first months they were open. I still have it. It too hasn't worn off at the elbows. I didn't get a friends and family discount. I suspect that would be impossible at Opening Ceremony, because I'm still trying to find someone who has met Humberto and Carol and doesn't consider them friends.

**CHRISTOPHER BOLLEN, WRITER AND EDITOR-AT-LARGE,
INTERVIEW MAGAZINE**

powerhouse

OPENING CEREMONY

Opening Ceremony Retail Conglomerate

Who are you?
The Opening Ceremony committee 2002. Opening
borrows certain key principles that Baron Pierre de
alleged founder of the modern-day Olympics, establ
Games. He pulled together ideas of anticipation, pa
celebration, and a host selection committee and co
an event that occurs on a systematic schedule. Ope
has adopted these ideas by focusing on one countr
finding elements of its artists, designers, corporate
and open-air markets in order to bring a sampling
sensation from that country back to the U.S. This is
"visiting collection" and takes up half the retail spec
houses U.S. designers, referred to as "home," and
made up of designers that will be part of our showr
located on the mezzanine. Referring back to the co
comprises various people from different fields and
for voting on the next country to visit
How many are on staff?
Two permanently, thirty contributors
When were you established, and why?
Opening Ceremony was registered as an LLC
on August 15, 2001.
What are you best known for?
Creating an open forum for people to turn idea
What are you working on?
Currently, opening Opening Ceremony New York
opening Opening Ceremony Los Angeles, Ope
San Francisco, Opening Ceremony Chicago, an
Ceremony Miami
What's your biggest motivating force?
Friends
Team motto Opening Ceremony or die!

Opening Ceremony, 35 Howard Street, NYC, 91
www.openingceremony.us

Photo: Harry, John, Jay, Keith, Rebecca, Eloise
Erin, Ian, Linda, Adam, Brooks, Lana, Shannon
Skaught, Shu, Case, Jenna, Holly, Ann, Sydney
the Opening Ceremony band

I was their first-ever customer. Take that where
you want to, I appreciate the guilt by association.

MICHAEL STIPE, MUSICIAN

**Michael Stipe photographed
by Terry Richardson, 2011.
LEFT PAGE:** Opening
Ceremony staff and friends
photographed by Leslie Kee
for *V Magazine*, 2002.

We made a line of instantly
popular sweatshirts that hinted
at collections to come!

Olivier Mosset, "Hoodie,"
2009. RIGHT PAGE:
Opening Ceremony
Diamond Hoodie, 2002.

In 2002, the diamond hoodie sweatshirt was the first garment made by Opening
Ceremony. With its simple graphic contrasting design, the sweatshirt was adopted
as a cult item by kids all over New York, who wear it to this day. Karl Lagerfeld even
wore one for an article in *V Magazine*, and the artist Olivier Mosset used the design
as the inspiration for his 2009 piece, "Hoodie." The sweatshirt's modern twist on a
familiar classic became a hallmark of the Opening Ceremony clothing collection,
which was launched the following year.

We design our Opening Ceremony collection in Chinatown and sell it around the world.

Opening Ceremony's collection, launched in spring 2003, captures the youthful, fun, and forward-thinking design aesthetic that defines the company as a whole. Opening Ceremony's line is designed in-house, and is inspired by a different traveling couple (brother/sister, boyfriend/girlfriend, best friends) each season. Composed of full menswear, womenswear, and accessories collections, the Opening Ceremony fashion label is now sold at over 200 stores worldwide. Characterized by a playful approach to dressing for every occasion, the collections have something for everyone. Opening Ceremony classics over the years have included the women's flare coat, the Gaudet babydoll dress, and much-loved knits and blazers for men. Shoes made in Portugal have become modern classics, with the M1 boot a go-to standard for many guys, and the Bumper Booties, Grunge sneakers, and Joelle clog boots are cult favorites for women. The Opening Ceremony art department designs many of the original prints in-house. Fans of the collection are legion, from Rihanna, Elijah Wood, and Kirsten Dunst, to the kids who work in the store.

Fabric trims and sketches by the Opening Ceremony design team.
LEFT PAGE: Opening Ceremony design studio.

2002 2003 2004 2005 2006

2008 2009 2010 2011 2012

Timeline of selected
Opening Ceremony
collection men's
and women's looks,
2002–2012.

OC Introduces Mary Ping

Mary Ping launched her eponymous line in 2001, and was one of the first designers stocked at Opening Ceremony, not to mention one of the original back room gang that chilled behind the register when the store first opened. With a thoroughly handmade ethos, her collection was developed in her family's Woodside, Queens, New York home. Mary Ping's deceptively simple clothing, with functional and intelligent design, won her the Ecco Domani award in 2005.

Mary Ping's current project is Slow and Steady Wins the Race, an experimental line of accessories. Reinterpreting and examining the way in which our culture lives with luxury, Slow and Steady puts an imaginative twist on iconic luxury pieces. With ironically ingenious pieces such as an Hermès bag remade in natural canvas, and a commitment to independence outside the relentless fashion cycle, Ping's critique of chic has matured alongside Opening Ceremony.

In the beginning years, Opening Ceremony was a clubhouse and a nice excuse to go hang out with friends. It was a total learning experience for everyone involved, and what was nice was the sort of honesty about it, about being green. Like, for instance, the time Carol called me and said, "Oh my God, Björk just bought your sweatshirt!" That sort of initial excitement. Slow and Steady Wins the Race is crafted on very specific design values. It was good to have a place where I could connect with people who shared this same philosophy.

MARY PING

Most of my hang time with those guys were family affairs involving a Korean or Chinese mom. This shared Asian heritage has been solid ground for bonding between us all. I know there are a lot of cool Asian Americans in New York City, but it's still nice to acknowledge when they are making the taste. Carol and Humberto were coming up at the same time the Yeah Yeah Yeahs were; at the top of the millennium, we had our little yellow fingers on the emerging downtown pulse when New York became white-hot again for a minute. The other day I was asking a friend about the wild success of the Opening Ceremony brand in the last decade, and that person said something like, "They love it and from the start they always stayed true to doing what they love." I'm sure there's more to it than that, but it makes sense that purity was the vibe back then. The thing about the NYC music scene back in the early 2000s was that the bands coming up had little-to-no expectation for success—nobody gave a shit about bands from NYC for years and years—the scene was flat soda. That gave us and a lot of other kids the freedom to go for broke and entertain ourselves—to make music to psych each other out. It was a fucking renaissance with seminal bands popping up all over boroughs. I'm pretty sure the attitude of "love it before you make it" had something to do with it.

KAREN O, MUSICIAN

Karen O at Opening Ceremony Los Angeles photographed by Lawrence K. Ho for the *Los Angeles Times*. LEFT PAGE: Slow and Steady Wins the Race rectangular canvas bag; Mary Ping FW05, photographed by Isabel Asha Penzlien.

Morrissey

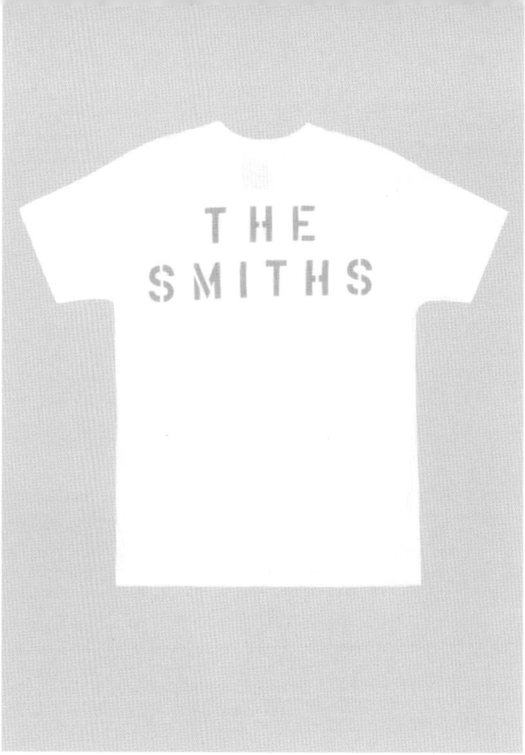

THE
SMITHS

AND IF THE
PEOPLE
STARE
THEN THE
PEOPLE
STARE

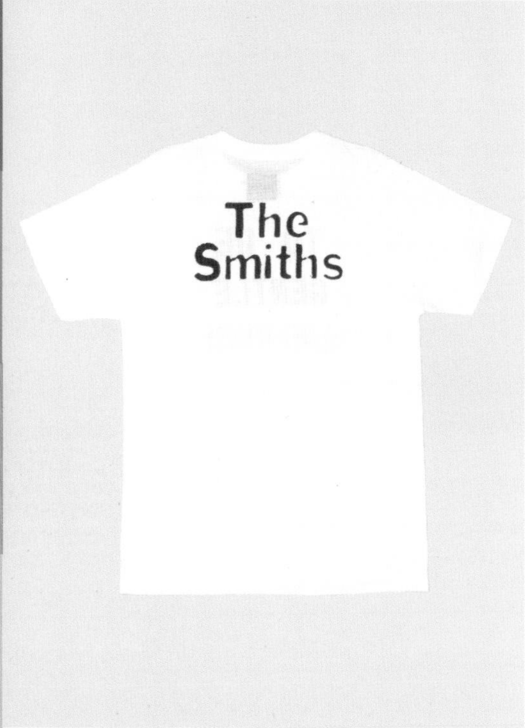

The
Smiths

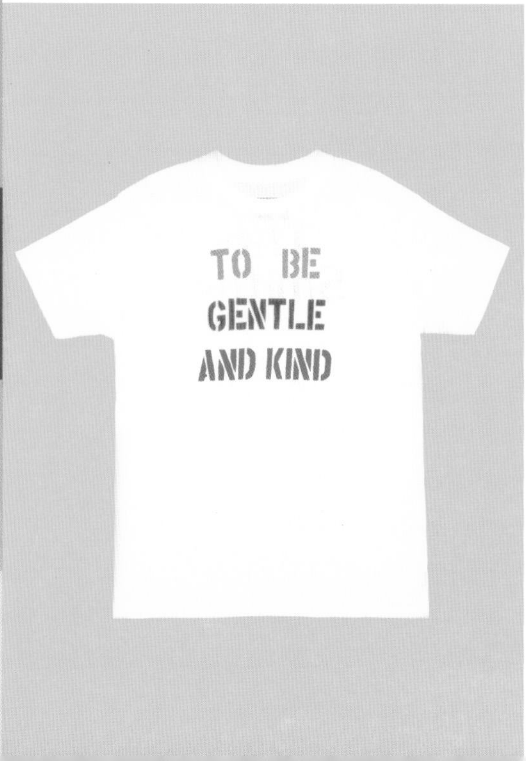

MORRISSEY

TO BE
GENTLE
AND KIND

TO SAY
THE SPECIAL
THINGS

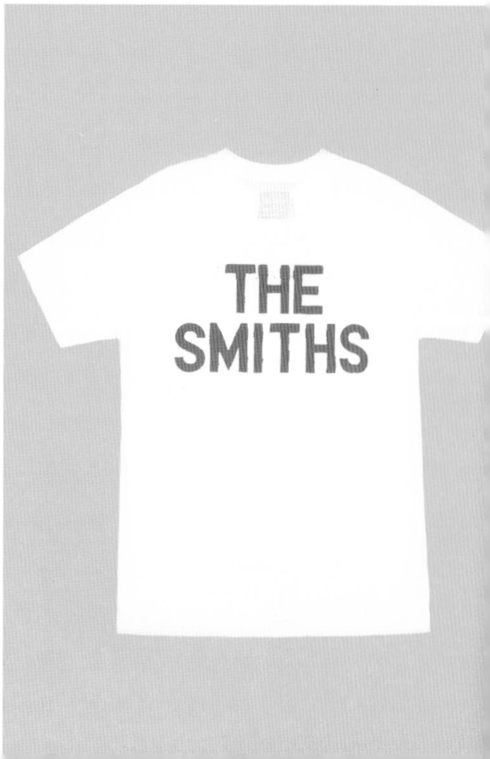

THE
SMITHS

OC × Marc Hundley

Canadian artist Marc Hundley installed a show of paper cutouts in the store, and an impromptu team of friends showed up to help make them, bringing back memories of cutting out paper snowflakes from kindergarten. Hundley's artwork often features songs and poems from our collective consciousness, both imaginary and real, with references to Rainer Maria Rilke, Joan Baez, and Morrissey. His work has always overlapped with the store, and his stenciled t-shirts with Smiths lyrics are Opening Ceremony favorites.

Marc Hundley's in-store exhibition and paper cut-outs. LEFT PAGE: Marc Hundley x Opening Ceremony t-shirts.

"So Bored" zine
photographed by
Zoë Ghertner, 2011.
RIGHT PAGE: "So
Bored" spreads.

We started a zine called "So Bored" because we were so bored!

Benjamin Cho, the fashion designer and early Opening Ceremony stalwart, put together the *So Bored* zine for Opening Ceremony, because we were *so* bored waiting for customers to come in that first year! For the zine, Ben asked anyone who stopped by the store to contribute their Top Ten list (of anything) and top three crushes. Leo Fitzpatrick and Benjamin Cho came up a lot as crush-worthy!

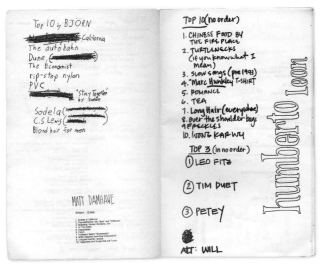

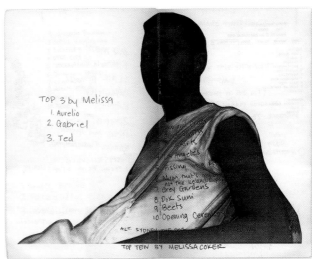

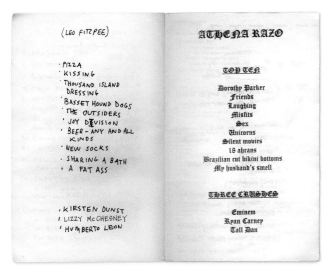

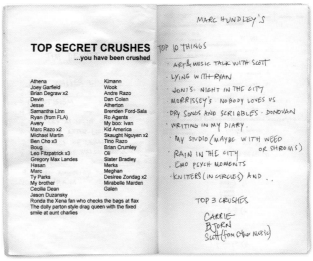

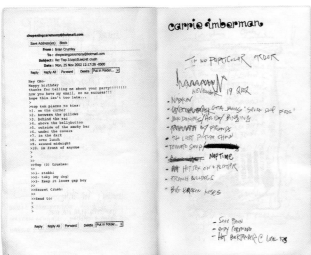

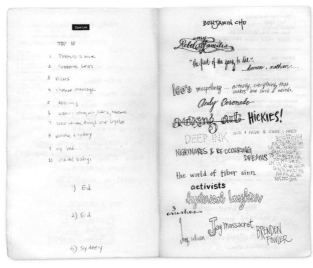

2003

BRAZIL

'03 BR

Olivia Kim photographed
by Terry Richardson, 2011.

Olivia Kim with Carol and Humberto on 2003

Carol and Humberto's closest friend, Olivia Kim, was one of Opening Ceremony's first employees, and she has seen the store develop from a downtown hangout spot into an international force in fashion. Now the vice president of creative for Opening Ceremony, Olivia manages everything from visual merchandising to collections and collaborations. She sat with her two best friends at Saturdays Surf, a neighborhood coffee spot where the trio reflected on ten years of Opening Ceremony's nonstop acceleration.

HUMBERTO: Olivia, you joined the store in 2003, the year of Brazil. You were one of our first employees!

OLIVIA: When I started, I had been in PR and consulting, and I had never really worked retail. You said, "We'll just hang out a few times a week in the store—you, me, and Carol." That's how it all started. The first day that I worked, we sold one sweatshirt. It was a $76 day. Then that weekend, since you finally had me to watch the store, you guys decided to take your first day off. I remember you said, "Don't worry, it won't be crazy." At a certain point I had to lock everybody in because there were so many people in the store and I couldn't do everything! I would have never imagined that ten years later we'd still be here.

CAROL: You've been with us the longest of any of our employees, and have really been responsible for the creative feel of it. How have you seen Opening Ceremony evolve?

OLIVIA: In the beginning, it was just the three of us hanging out as friends and working. When you work in a store with people who are really creative, you're eager to do new things to not become bored. We just kept bouncing ideas off of each other. The most amazing thing about Humberto is that he often says, "What do you mean 'what if'? Let's just do it!"

HUMBERTO: That is how a lot of it developed at the beginning. We started our own line and showroom in the year or so after you arrived.

OLIVIA: We were selling our product so quickly that we had to start our own line of sweatshirts. This Japanese buyer came in who wanted to buy our sweatshirts for his store, which is what pushed us to start the showroom officially in early 2003. And now of course our showroom reps 25 international brands.

CAROL: In 2003, we traveled to Brazil so many times to check out what was going on there. We were really taken with the country.

OLIVIA: Nobody had done anything with Brazilian fashion before that. We could do it with fresh eyes and change any expectations that people had about Brazil. At that point, all people thought about with Brazil were cows and parades and Rio. They didn't realize that there were these really talented people doing cool things. The creativity down there is incredible. I think it's part of that Brazilian culture—this very warm, loving, textured community.

HUMBERTO: Yes, it's something that we appreciated. Coming from New York, it was easy to bring that energy back and translate it.

CAROL: The first time we went, it was really as people who love to travel, and we were open to everything—the supermarket, the food carts, the traffic.

OLIVIA: Going down there to look at the fashion was pretty amazing. There were these designers like Alexandre Herchcovitch and Gloria Coelho. They were like the Marc Jacobs of Brazil; they were so big yet no one had heard of them here. Alexandre Herchcovitch was designing all the uniforms for the McDonald's in Brazil at the time.

HUMBERTO: And the response in New York to all these Brazilian brands was so positive.

OLIVIA: I think people were really surprised. Buyers were asking about the designers, so we brought Alexandre Herchcovitch, Lorenzo Merlino, and Neon into the showroom. We developed a kind of broken English language with them. We helped them grow these Brazilian brands into worldwide brands.

CAROL: And of course we brought Havaianas to America for the first time. We just saw everyone wearing these brightly colored flip-flops and thought they were amazing. And nobody here had heard of them.

OLIVIA: Right, they were in these supermarket chains called Extra. It was like *Supermarket Sweep*—we would fill these shopping carts! One of us filled it with just Havaianas and another would fill it with these peanut butter candies that we liked.

HUMBERTO: Brazil was the first country where we started fine-tuning our radar, so that we could pick up on what was going on there at the time.

OLIVIA: I think it's just pure emotion. I think a lot of it has to do with us genuinely loving fashion as kids: being interested in what we were wearing to school, what was happening in the magazines at the time, and pop culture—it's about being nostalgic. It wasn't about going there to find out what was cool. It was more of, "I love this, and somebody in New York is going to love this too." ▶

CAROL: Those Brazil trips were the first time we really traveled together. And we've been traveling together ever since.

OLIVIA: I have to say that the three of us travel really well together as a group. Carol is always concerned about the food, what the first thing we're going to eat will be. Humberto always wants to shop right away. And he can go out every night—but that's true in New York, too. That's one of the best things about Humberto: he doesn't want to miss a thing. Just keeping up with him is a full-time job. Carol is similar, but in a much calmer way. She maps things out a lot more. Spike Jonze asked me if I'm more of an "Humberto" or a "Carol." I sometimes feel like I'm your child; I have the personalities of both of you.

CAROL: I can totally see that. So 2003 was the year the New York blackout happened. Since so many people congregated at the store that day, it's really when I started thinking of Opening Ceremony not just as a store, but also as a community for creative, downtown people.

OLIVIA: Opening Ceremony has always been home base. At the beginning, the backroom had people working on their own creative projects: zines, PR, writing…. This was a place where we could come and bounce ideas off of people. I don't think this has changed at all. Opening Ceremony is a collective where creative people can come, and I think that that magnetism has spread to not only designers, but also to musicians, actors, filmmakers, and artists. And I think that the most exciting thing about where we are now is that the group and community is so big.

HUMBERTO: It is really gratifying. In 2003, we started having these awesome concerts in the store. Mark Gardener from Ride, and then Lisa Lisa and the Cult Jam performed at one of our parties. I often wonder what it is that unites all these people, whether it's Andrew Kuo or Ratatat or Wong Kar-wai or Chloë or Rodarte.

OLIVIA: I think the most unifying trait or spirit is this idea that you can be a part of something that you know has no limits; you know that you have the support and room for creativity. There's something very magnetic about that.

CAROL: Totally. And in 2003, we were all starting to find each other and create this creative community. That year Ben Cho, Paul Sevigny, and Brian DeGraw started Smiths Night at Sway. Ryan McGinley was the youngest person to have a solo show at the Whitney.

OLIVIA: Yes. It's like New York was suddenly mirroring what we wanted to do and see. I don't think anybody plans for these things to happen, these cultural movements. To us it was just, "Oh, our friend Ryan has a show at the Whitney. Holy shit!" At the time we genuinely wanted to support our friend—it was all genuine. None of that group mentality was contrived. We wanted to dance to Morrissey on Sunday nights with all our friends. So we did. ◆

2003 BRAZIL : SAO PAULO

RITZ
YOU'LL BEA PROBABLY RUN INTO SOMEONE YOU KNOW AT THIS COZY NEIGHBORHOOD RESTAURANT.
ALAMEDA FRANCA, 1088, JARDINS

CLUBE ALÔCA
SUPER FUN TRANNY CLUB!
RUA FREI CANECA, 916, BELA VISTA
aloca.com.br

D.EDGE D. EDGE
STILL A FUN PLACE TO DANCE THE NIGHT AWAY.
AVENIDA AURO SOARES DE MOURA ANDRADE, 141, BARRA FUNDA
d-edge.com.br

FEIRA DA PRAÇA BENEDITO CALIXTO
AN AMAZING FLEA MARKET WHERE WE LOVE TO SNACK ON COXINHAS (FRIED SHREDDED CHICKEN IN BATTER) AND PÃO DEQUEIJOS (CHEESE BREAD)
PRAÇA BENEDITO CALIXTO, PINHEIROS

CONSULADO MINEIRO
DELICIOUS HOMESTYLE DISHES. LOVE THE FEISÃO TROPEIRO, A BEAN STEW WITH PORK FAT, BACON, AND MANIOC FLOUR.
PRAÇA BENEDICTO CALIXTO, 74, PINHEIROS

2004

MAVE
GREA
CLOTHI
KNA
BERN
63-6

BALL
CLASS
+ DA
BET
AVEN
MITT
ball

HUM
YO
BUT
TREA
IT
FRA
FRIE
hum

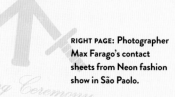

OC Introduces
Alexandre Herchcovitch

A true international original, Alexandre Herchcovitch was one of the first designers from Brazil to be carried at Opening Ceremony. Discovered on one of Carol and Humberto's first trips to São Paolo, Herchcovitch was already a pioneer in the country and a must for inclusion in the year of Brazil. In the years since, he has gained fame and notoriety while continuing to surprise with always avant-garde collections, which usually include his signature skull motifs and religious imagery.

Based in São Paolo, and definitively part of the Brazilian fashion underground since his start in 1993, Herchcovitch has shown his collections in Paris, London, and New York, and is something of a cult figure in Japan. His work remains challenging with an increasingly elegant yet genre-bending and experimental approach. Whether he is creating uniforms for Brazil's McDonald's restaurants or couture-like runway looks, Herchcovitch always approaches fashion with a sense of humor.

Opening Ceremony is responsible for showing the world that Brazil is much more than Carnival, samba, and Rio de Janeiro.

ALEXANDRE HERCHCOVITCH

Carol and Humberto were roaming around Brazil and discovered these amazingly durable, stylish, and delightful Havaianas flip-flops. Since 1962, Havaianas has been making the same footwear, inspired by the rice straw-soled Japanese Zori sandal, hence the textured rice pattern of the foot-bed. The two Opening Ceremony founders decided they couldn't live without them and became the first store to carry the shoes in the US. They went back to Brazil 16 times that year to fill orders that had grown to the magnitude of thousands per month. The year Opening Ceremony featured Brazilian designers truly brought Brazilian fashion and style to the forefront, increasing awareness for Brazilian design aesthetics and fashion designers and brands. As a result, Havaianas has grown explosively in the US.

JIM ANSTEY, MARKETING DIRECTOR, HAVAIANAS

Havaianas flip-flops photographed by Zoë Ghertner, 2011. LEFT PAGE: Alexandre Herchcovitch SS05, photographed by Marcio Madeira.

Humberto is the only guy I ever kissed —
oh, and my first Asian.

LEO FITZPATRICK, ACTOR

Leo Fitzpatrick and Chrissie
Miller photographed by
Terry Richardson, 2011.
RIGHT PAGE: Opening
Ceremony Showroom
photographed by Michael
Vahrenwald, 2012.

We opened a showroom that represents amazing designers from around the world.

Opening Ceremony Showroom was founded in 2003 as a logical extension of the business. With designers from off-the-grid countries needing representation, and with retailers eager to discover them, Opening Ceremony became the link between these brands and the international retail landscape. The Centre Street showroom space in New York currently represents over twenty international and American designers, including men's and women's ready-to-wear, and offers a platform for these designers to grow their own businesses. Most of the collections by brands such as Pamela Love, Delfina Delettrez, Patrik Ervell, and Suno (plus Opening Ceremony's house lines) are carried in the Opening Ceremony retail boutiques for at least a season when they make it to the showroom, further expanding the idea of Opening Ceremony as a multi-faceted, all-inclusive environment.

When I started Sophomore, I showed the line to so many different showrooms and no one seemed to get it. When they asked us to join the Opening Ceremony Showroom, I was so excited that I could have cried!

CHRISSIE MILLER, SOPHOMORE

OC × Andrew Kuo

New York Artist Andrew Kuo has been an integral part of the Opening Ceremony universe since its inception. Best known for his gorgeous charts documenting the minutiae of the music scene for *The New York Times*, he also paints, writes, and blogs for Opening Ceremony. In collaboration with Opening Ceremony, Andrew showcased a capsule line of t-shirts that featured two persistent obsessions, New York and pizza, punctuated with googly eyes.

At a little after 4 pm on Thursday, August 14, 2003, the power went out in my studio. The place was a dump—we were frequently subjected to power outages, water leaks, and broken elevators. I walked outside to wait for something to happen, as I usually did, but that day I wasn't alone. Everyone had also gone black. As far as we knew, the whole city and world didn't exist past what we could see—there was no way to tell. We stood still, in the street, peering around as far as we could see to make sure it wasn't just us. Without thinking, I started walking toward Opening Ceremony.

In the winters after that, Carol, Humberto, and a few of us would spend entire Saturday and Sunday afternoons in the back of 35 Howard. To pass time, we made little books of drawings. We ate hot soups together at a table littered with plastic forks and piles of unworn clothes. Humberto would chase shoplifters through the snow and Carol would mention that she loved the song that was on right then. In the summers, we would sit on the stoop and fantasize about rooftop barbeques and laugh about last night's proceedings. We would just say things we felt like saying. Things grew and changed and we all went on to whatever we went on to do, but Opening Ceremony has never been far away.

ANDREW KUO

TOP: Andrew Kuo; BOTTOM: T-shirts by Andrew Kuo for Opening Ceremony. RIGHT PAGE: "Blackout, Candle" by Andrew Kuo, inspired by the 2003 New York Blackout, 2011. FOLLOWING SPREAD: "Ten Years of a NYC Life at Night, or, Life's Short But So Am I (Open Book)" by Andrew Kuo, 2012.

2002 2003 2004 2005 2006

TEN YEARS OF A NYC LIFE AT NIGHT
OR
LIFE'S SHORT BUT SO AM I (OPEN BOOK)

PLACES

Max Fish
Uncle Ming's
The Hole
Sway
Peasant
St Dymphna's

Lit
Avenue
Bacaro
The Jane
Santos Party House
Clandestino
The Westway

2007 2008 2009 2010 2011 2012

It's much harder regretting something you didn't do than regretting something you did do.
All my friends need to know how important they are in the universe!!! (Right after these four beers.)
Everything good happens from 2AM to 4AM, and by "good" I mean two hour debates about vitamins.
I hope everyone's wild and youthful days also involve listening to only The _____ for hours.
The "walk of shame" is actually not that shameful when you have a grilled cheese in your hand.
We can't look back and laugh if we don't stay up until 6:12AM and smash those bottles right now.
I think about and miss you more than you'll ever know.

We love dancing with our friends, especially at Sway's Smiths Night!

For nearly a decade, the extended Opening Ceremony family could be found every Sunday night, dancing to The Smiths at Sway, on the western edge of SoHo. Started in 2003 by Benjamin Cho, Paul Sevigny, and Gang Gang Dance's Brian DeGraw, Smiths Night grew from a geeky Morrissey fest with a few friends into a New York nightlife standby. No one who attended will forget the Halloween in 2006 when there was a Morrissey look-alike contest—skateboarding photographer Patrick O'Dell won, but Ryan McGinley came in a close second as Zombie Moz. Looking for an alternative to overblown velvet-roped club nights, the Sway gang concocted a party where 80s and 90s teenage bedroom music would reign and everyone who went felt like part of the club.

TOP: Carol at Sway, 2004; **CENTER:** the DJ booth at Sway, photographed by Maryam L'Ange; **BOTTOM:** Ryan McGinley, Humberto, Keith Gonzalez, and Esteban Arboleta at Sway, 2004.

The best thing about Smiths Night was when Brian DeGraw wouldn't play the fuckin' Smiths. Although I do have to say that it is a comfort to hear them at times when you're in that drunken haze.

LIZZI BOUGATSOS, SINGER, GANG GANG DANCE

Lizzi Bougatsos
photographed by Terry
Richardson, 2011.
FOLLOWING SPREAD:
Opening Ceremony
SS03, photographed by
Isabel Asha Penzlien.

Opening Ceremony
est. 2002

CLOTHING AND ACCESSORIES

Home Team (US): Benjamin Cho, Cloak, Opening Ceremony, Rachel Comey, Indigo People, Rikki Kasso, Faunae, Mary Ping, Will Lemon III, Saved, Kitterick, Oi, IN Magazine and select vintage

Visiting Team (Brazil): Fabia Bercsek, Walerio Araujo, Erika Ikezili, Jefferson de Assis, Simone Nunes, Alexandre Herchcovitch, Eduardo Inagaki, Calota Joakina, Havaianna, Reinaldo Lourenco, Lorenzo Merlino, Neon, Fanzine 2

35 HOWARD STREET NEW YORK, NY 10013 t212 2192688 f212 219 2637
openingceremony.us

2004

GERMANY

Ryan McGinley
photographed by Terry
Richardson, 2011.

Ryan McGinley with Carol and Humberto on 2004

Carol and Humberto sat down with photographer Ryan McGinley at Opening Ceremony's Centre Street office to discuss downtown creativity over the past ten years. The youngest photographer to have a solo show at the Whitney Museum (he was 25 when the show opened in 2003), Ryan has photographed everything from desert road trips to Morrissey's fans. From the outset, Ryan has also been linked with fellow artists, and Opening Ceremony friends, Dan Colen and the late Dash Snow as leading the latest generation of downtown New York creativity. In 2004, Ryan created a limited-edition box set of postcards for the store, and he has since collaborated on several other projects. He spoke to Carol and Humberto about their shared love of Morrissey, the Olympics, and their deep abiding passion for the downtown New York they have come of age in together.

RYAN: Why did you feature Germany in 2004?

HUMBERTO: A lot of it had to do with the big art movement that was happening in Berlin. Carol and I were being selfish and wanted to travel to places we thought were cool, and Germany was one of those places.

CAROL: A lot of the people we knew were moving there and getting studio spaces.

HUMBERTO: We wanted to know more about what was going on, and ended up going 12 times that year. That's when we first carried Bless and all the German stuff, including classic brands like Shiesser, the old underwear line.

RYAN: I modeled for Bless in Milan in 2004. I wore this acid jean top and bottom, and they poured flour all over me. What else happened in 2004? I went to a lot of Morrissey shows. We went to Miami, Tennessee, and a bunch of other places in the South, Tulsa, and Philly. I remember Chloë jumping on stage in Philly and hugging Morrissey—it was crazy!

HUMBERTO: Did you get kicked out?

RYAN: We didn't, because everyone does that during the show. But she actually jumped the barrier and was screaming at the top of her lungs, "FUCK YES!" It was so good!

CAROL: Where did you hang out in 2004?

RYAN: 2004, for me, was kind of the end of an era, because I was in the East Village for seven years before that. And that's where I met my friends, where we all hung out. It was all about The Cock, Lit, and The Hole. I was living with Dan Colen and he needed to get a studio to paint, so we found our Canal Street studio and moved there. That was the year Dash Snow moved from Avenue C to the Bowery. And that was when he started making art. We had these long conversations about making art and that's when he started making collages. Do you remember your party where Dash tagged the roof? I brought Dash to Humberto's party and the first thing that he does is go on the roof and tags someone's window. I was like, "Oh my god! Dude, you're destroying me!"

HUMBERTO: The entire hallway was tagged by the end of the party. That apartment later became Proenza Schouler's office and, after that, Joseph Altuzarra's office. It was a cool space, and I'd have these random parties there.

RYAN: I went on a trip to Mexico where Patrik Ervell came and basically had a bunch of models with him. That trip was one of the first times where I casted for my photographs, because before then I was just photographing my friends. I also went to Australia where I had some exhibitions. At the last minute, Waris Ahluwalia and Natasha Lyonne showed up at the airport and decided to come with me. I remember being on the plane with Natasha while everyone was sleeping. I looked over and Natasha had a cigarette in her mouth! She smiled at me, lit the cigarette, and took three drags. It was so cinematic because she had the overhead light on her. It was the craziest thing I've ever seen.

HUMBERTO: That is pretty badass.

RYAN: Dan and Dash did a lot of those hamster nests. It was right when the Maritime Hotel had just opened, and we got a room there and had an insane party where everyone was tripping with every drug possible. We shredded every phone book in the Maritime and I thought I was on a ship, and then regretted it the next day because I was trying to be professional.

HUMBERTO: I almost felt like it was a time of false adulthood where you had to kind of be professional but not really....

RYAN: It was like going from *The Breakfast Club* to *The Big Chill*.

CAROL: We definitely felt that cusp-of-growing-up thing.

RYAN: One of the things that I really hate is when people say that New York is not what it used to be because you know what? New York is always cool. There's always something going on. You run into old timers who will say that it's not what it used to be. I don't know man, but I don't believe in that. And I'm sure people you've interviewed have probably said ▶

that—you should punch them in the face! Because New York is still happening. Everything is still so exciting.

CAROL: Definitely. After traveling so much it's made me appreciate New York so much more, because there really is no city like it in the world.

HUMBERTO: What are your thoughts about Opening Ceremony and how it's evolved?

RYAN: You guys created a subculture. I think it's interesting. When I was younger it was about Supreme, Liquid Sky, and X-Girl—those were the things in the 90s that I identified with. I wore their clothes and said "this is who I am." I think that's what Opening Ceremony does for a new generation. I feel so proud that we came up together and are making our impact in a larger way.

HUMBERTO: Also in the last ten years, it felt like it was easy to do anything. Let's do a make-out party! Let's make a zine called *So Bored,* because we are so bored! I think all of these things came out of just wanting to do something.

RYAN: I feel strongly about it being downtown. It's an adventure. When I have to go uptown I feel like I'm going to panic. Being here, with you guys, right now on Centre Street, I feel like nothing's changed. I've been hanging out downtown for 20 years and everything we talked about has pretty much happened downtown over the last decade. It's not just New York, it's downtown. ◆

2004 GERMANY : BERLIN

MAUER PARK FLEA MARKET

GREAT SECOND HAND CLOTHING & KNICK KNACKS.
BERNAUER STRASSE 63-64, MITTE

BALLHAUS MITTE

CLASSIC GERMAN DISHES + DANCING ... WHAT'S BETTER?
AUGUST STRASSE 24, MITTE
ballhausmitte.de

HUMANA SECOND HAND

YOU HAVE TO DIG, BUT THE OCCASIONAL TREASURE MAKES IT WORTH IT.
FRANKFURTER TOR 3, FRIEDRICHSHAIN
humana-second-hand.de

ANDREAS MURKUDIS.

HIGHLY CURATED DESIGNER SHOP.
POTSDAMER STRASSE 81E, TIERGATEN
andreasmurkudis.com

THE SNAKE CASTLE

AN ODD MAGICAL STORE OWNED BY NEW YORK EX PATS AND FILLED WITH 90's STICKERS, CRYSTALS AND MORE
BOXHAGENER STRASSE, 117, FRIEDRICHSHAIN
thesnakecastle.com

2005

HER
ONE
GAL
WOR
2 k
BET
heral

THE V
SPECIA
FROM
ERA
14 BA
BRICK
vintag

LISBO
YOU M
CUSTA
THE
DELICI
57 Q
KENS

Patrik Ervell and Ryan McGinley photographed by Ryan McGinley, 2004.
RIGHT PAGE: "Olympic Swimmers" by Ryan McGinley, originally published in the August 8, 2004 edition of *The New York Times*, collected into a postcard set by Opening Ceremony for the Nike Souvenir exhibition, 2004.

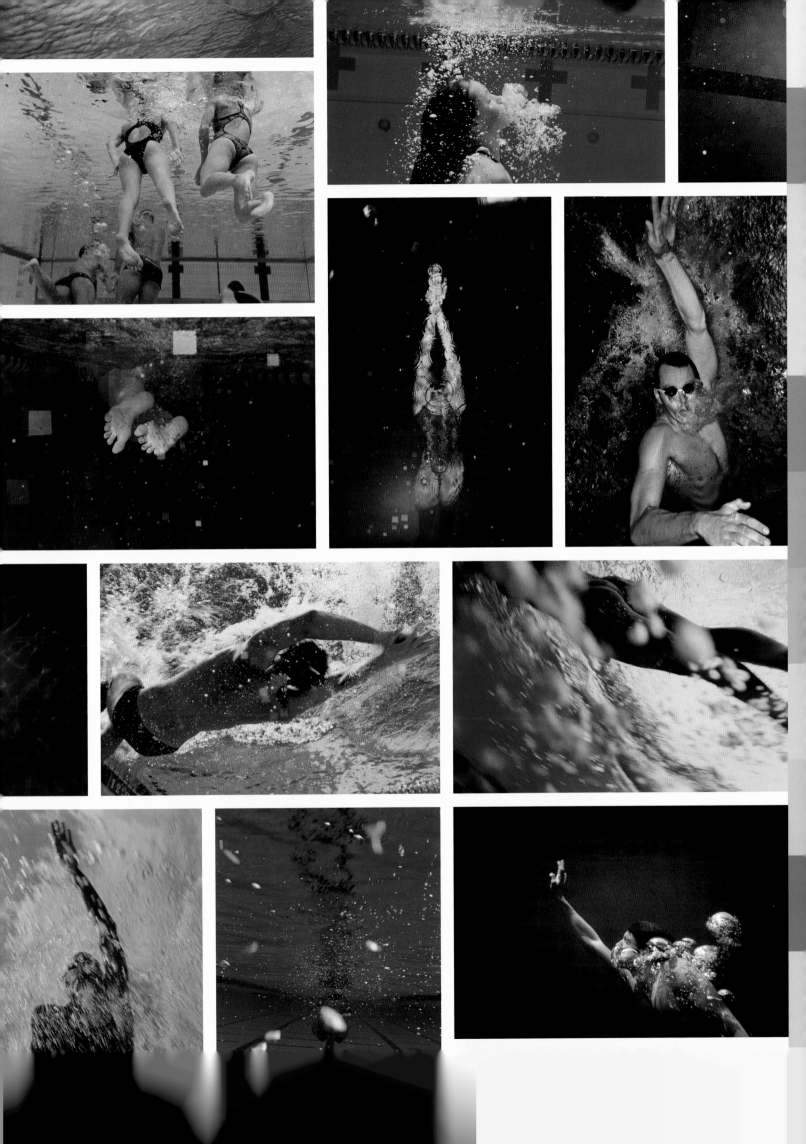

OC × Nike Souvenir

Opening Ceremony joined forces with Nike to produce Souvenir, a collection in which designers and artists were paired to reimagine Nike products. Designers and artists such as Mary Ping, Bless, and Wendy and Jim recreated Nike designs with an original, artistic take. Alexandre Herchcovitch dipped a pair of Air Max Ones in black rubber, and Andrew Kuo silkscreened a wooden basketball box. As Mary Ping noted, the Souvenir project was an early precursor to the ethos of collaboration that Opening Ceremony would later become known for.

Nike and Opening Ceremony seem at first like radically different brands, but both were founded with a sort of bicameral attitude that elevates innovation on the one hand and a commitment to lightness of spirit on the other. Nike made its name in the 80s by combining great products, great collaborators, and a sense of humor in a way that produced both iconic products and iconic cultural moments, such as Michael Jordan and Spike Lee or Bo Jackson and Bo Diddley. Similarly, Carol and Humberto have developed the Opening Ceremony brand with an amazing aptitude for introducing innovative fashion to a larger audience without forgetting to make it fun—whether through memorable events such as Ratatat's in-store performance, collaborations such as the 2004 Souvenir collection, or the shop's many playful online videos.

SHU HUNG, MARKETING LEAD, NIKE

Store installation views, Nike Souvenir exhibition, photographed by Isabel Asha Penzlien, 2004.

'04 DE

OC Introduces Schiesser...

Carol and Humberto discovered iconic German underwear company Schiesser on a trip to Berlin, after Schiesser Revival was introduced in 2003 to bring back classic pieces from the original company, founded in 1875. The Revival collections recall Schiesser styles from the 20s through the 50s, using some of the original fabrics while introducing new colors into the mix. Carol and Humberto immediately fell in love with Schiesser's eye for detail: from its use of soft and nostalgic fabrics to the thoughtful packaging of each item. Schiesser boxes are now stacked high in every Opening Ceremony stockroom, and more than a few hunky actors (who we can't name!) are fans of the boxer briefs.

Bless...

Established in 1996 and based in both Paris and Berlin, Bless takes conceptual design to its highest level. With experimental pieces such as a combination boot/socks, as well as an electrical products line featuring radios and cords dressed in leather and cloth, Bless has always been whimsically outside the mainstream fashion world. In addition to beauty products and home furnishings, Bless has also exhibited their particular blend of art, home concepts, and ready-to-wear clothing at contemporary art venues such as the Centre Pompidou in Paris, the Berlin Biennale, and the Kunsthalle in Basel. Fashion design legend Martin Margiela picked up their outlandish fur wigs to use in his Fall 1997 collection, catapulting the unique Bless take on fashion to a larger audience.

...and Bernhard Willhelm

Bernhard Willhelm's universe has always been intensely playful and otherworldly. After graduating from the Royal Academy of Fine Arts in Antwerp in 1998, he showed his first collection at Paris Fashion Week the following year. Each season, he brings to light a new palette of explosive colors and prints, which have included photographs, geometric shapes, cosmic starbursts, reworked corporate logos, tribal designs from imaginary lands, and even classic stripes and plaids, all produced in technicolor hues. In the early 2000s, Bernhard's printed sweatshirts were all over the streets of Berlin, not to mention on the Opening Ceremony crew. Ever since, Bernhard's shows in Paris have always been on the agenda of the OC buyers.

But Bernhard Willhelm's world does not end at fashion. Along with his partner Jutta Kraus, he has exhibited artworks at museums and galleries that blend fashion with the surreal, such as sculptures of skeletons smoking joints and two-headed men adrift in swampy gardens while dressed in typically dreamy Bernhard Willhelm outfits.

Bernhard Willhelm SS12, photographed by Helene Bozzi. LEFT PAGE, CLOCKWISE FROM TOP LEFT: Schiesser photographed for Opening Ceremony; Bless hairbrush and installation photographed by Bless. FOLLOWING SPREAD: Opening Ceremony FW04, photographed by Isabel Asha Penzlien.

2005

UNITED KINGDOM

Brian Phillips photographed
by Terry Richardson, 2011.

Brian Phillips with Carol and Humberto on 2005

Brian Phillips has been an integral part of Opening Ceremony since its outset. In the years since opening his first office in the store's basement, Brian has grown his PR firm, Black Frame, in tandem with Opening Ceremony, while helping promote the brand's growth at every step. With clients such as the Frieze Art Fair, Fondazione Prada, Nike, and Rodarte, Black Frame has become a leader in the branding of some of the most respected fashion and culture brands of our time. The three longtime collaborators got together in Paris to talk about the past ten years, going from downtown to the world stage, and the importance of a good party.

BRIAN: When Humberto and Carol opened OC, I remember stuffing foam into the purple pillows and helping put together the chandelier, which had a million pieces to put together. I was at *Visionaire* at the time.

HUMBERTO: And then a year after we opened we acquired our basement space, which used to be a massage parlor. You became our first tenant, with your PR/production company at the time.

BRIAN: I would work in the basement in a cubicle. Basically, every other hour I would come upstairs to smoke cigarettes and chitchat with you two in the back office.

HUMBERTO: The backroom was where we would invite everyone. Leo Fitzpatrick would come and use the fax machine to have his scripts for *The Wire* sent over. People would come into the backroom to do taxes together because Carol would have advice on what to claim. Kirsten Dunst and Jake and Maggie Gyllenhaal would come by to shop and say hi.

BRIAN: In 2004, I opened Black Frame and moved down to Broome Street. And in 2005, Opening Ceremony became my client. That was the year things started blowing up. Why did you guys decide to feature the United Kingdom that year?

CAROL: We read that Anna Wintour was skipping the London shows. At that time, a lot of the big British designers were showing in Paris, from Stella McCartney to Alexander McQueen. Carol and I figured that there must be young designers still in London. We brainstormed a list of designers to see, including Marios Schwab, Richard Nicoll, Gareth Pugh, and Peter Jensen.

HUMBERTO: We went to an abandoned building to see the Gareth Pugh collection. We thought none of his clothes were wearable. He said, "Just give me 5,000 pounds and I'll make

stuff." And that's how we bought his collection: we gave him money and he sent us whatever he could.

BRIAN: And that was the counterpoint to Topshop, which you launched in America that year. It was already a major cult high street brand in Britain. The Topshop launch at Opening Ceremony sold out in a day and a half. It was out of control. It was the first thing that connected Opening Ceremony to the mass understanding of fashion.

CAROL: The year we featured London was the first time we felt defined. Having Topshop as well as these emerging designers was a very strong message.

BRIAN: That became the whole concept of Opening Ceremony.

CAROL: Another big moment was when we opened the Cloak store in our Greene Street space. We had always thought about opening a shop for another brand. We sold Cloak in our store and had developed a clientele for it, so we decided to open the shop with its designer Alexandre Plokhov. We always knew that would be part of our business model: to build a brand and help them realize the retail concept.

BRIAN: I've learned a lot about doing business by working with you, and a lot about communication and throwing parties. Parties have always been a large part of Opening Ceremony.

CAROL: It's an extension of the store, like the back office blown up to a bigger level. The parties are always crazy and fun—everyone dancing their heart out.

HUMBERTO: I think people tend to remember the crazier, bigger parties like the Slits concert at Webster Hall for Chloë Sevigny's first collection; but we also hosted the record release show for the first Ratatat album and a Wong Kar-wai signing. It was never promoting anything—we were just promoting fun. The first party we ever had at the store was for my 26th birthday, right before it opened. Someone was spray painting in the back office—it was out of control.

CAROL: It bombed. People were smoking and leaving cigarettes butts on the floor and alcohol was everywhere. Our moms were guarding the merchandise.

HUMBERTO: But that dedication to fun is part of what I feel has always set us apart from other fashion stores and fashion brands.

BRIAN: I wouldn't even call it a fashion brand. It is defining a place where people interested in fashion, nightlife, art, and music can come together with a common ground. Plus, everyone is so cute. I feel like people come to Opening Ceremony to check people out. ◆

OC introduces Marios Schwab...

Fashion talents like Marios Schwab first got Carol and Humberto excited to showcase the United Kingdom in 2005. The Greco-Austrian designer set up his own line that same year, and his impeccably tailored, thigh-skimming dresses were immediately creating a buzz. By the following year, Marios was being hailed as the poster boy for a new generation of London designers, and was rewarded with Best New Designer at the British Fashion Awards.

Ever since graduating ESMOD in Berlin, and later Central Saint Martins in London, the designer's approach has been form-and body-centric, making him the perfect choice for the creative directorship at disco-era design house Halston from 2009 to 2011. While Marios' inspirations range from anatomical manuals to corsetry, pinups to power women, each season his precise cuts and darkly romantic sentiment will make jaws drop along the runway.

'05 UK

I remember going in to the store years ago, after a breakup, to try on a sexy black Marios Schwab dress, and Humberto was like, "Whoa—you have breasts?! I've never seen them. Buy the dress, you'll get back together!" Nope. But I still love the dress. And the advice.

MIRABELLE MARDEN, PHOTOGRAPHER

2005 UNITED KINGDOM : LONDON

HERALD ST
ONE OF OUR FAVORITE GALLERIES IN THE WORLD!
2 HERALD STREET, BETHNAL GREEN
heraldst.com

THE VINTAGE EMPORIUM
SPECIALTY VINTAGE FROM THE VICTORIAN ERA & '50's.
14 BACON STREET, BRICK LANE
vintageemporiumcafe.com

LISBOA PÂTISSERIE
YOU HAVE TO TRY THEIR CUSTARD TARTS! AND THEIR ESPRESSO IS DELICIOUS.
57 GOLBORNE ROAD, KENSINGTON

LA FROMAGERIE
AMAZING CHEESE SELECTION WITH A DELICIOUS CAFE IN THE BACK.
2-6 MOXON STREET, MARYLEBONE
lafromagerie.co.uk

NELSONS HEAD
ITS THE KIND OF PUB WHERE YOU WILL RUN INTO A FRIEND, WHICH IS SO NICE
32 HORATIO STREET, SHOREDITCH
nelsonshead.com

RELLIK
AMAZING VINTAGE
8 GOLBORNE ROAD, KENSINGTON
relliklondon.co.uk

OPENING CEREMONY
Est. 2002

...and Gareth Pugh

Gareth Pugh was working from an abandoned building in 2005 when he staged a private runway show of his first collection for Carol and Humberto. They filmed the spectacle on an early digital point-and-shoot, and the images are pretty much illegible apart from a blurry shaking and constant oohs and ahhs. After this makeshift presentation, Opening Ceremony snapped up the young designer right away. Since then, the designer's processions of distorted forms and sci-fi silhouettes have united scenesters and critics in an awe-struck agreement about Pugh's genius, earning him fashion's ANDAM award in 2008.

Gareth grew up in Sunderland in the North of England, and graduated from Central Saint Martins in 2003. The designer's taste for theatrics has defined his creations throughout his career. Sharply-angled headpieces, coats that light up, and a wardrobe of showpieces for Kylie Minogue have all starred in Gareth's ongoing performance. Pugh's evolution has taken on the form of redefined luxury, with cashmere, leather, and fur adding a tactile dimension to his fashion cubism.

Gareth Pugh SS12, photographed by Chris Moore/Catwalking.com. LEFT PAGE: Marios Schwab FW11, photographed for Opening Ceremony.

OC Introduces Topshop

Opening Ceremony was the first American retailer to carry cult British high street brand Topshop. What was once known as "Peter Robinson's Top Shop," Topshop grew from the basement of a Sheffield department store in 1964 to become the world's largest fashion chain, spreading its influence from England's high streets into Europe and across Asia. We couldn't have been happier to bring over this British institution, which has collaborated with the likes of Kate Moss and championed many of our favorite British designers, including Christopher Kane, Marios Schwab, and Mary Katrantzou.

American fashion fanatics had been making the pilgrimage to Oxford Street for years before they could get their fix stateside, and when Topshop arrived at 35 Howard Street, pandemonium ensued, as fashion editors, high school kids, and pretty much everyone else flocked to the store for the launch. Topshop must have liked the neighborhood, as it now has a full American flagship store up the street on Broadway.

'05 UK

Topshop at Opening Ceremony. RIGHT PAGE: Kate Moss for Topshop shirt photographed by Zoë Ghertner, 2011.

After going to London just to shop
at Topshop, it was so nice to buy those
clothes in dollars and not pounds!

HONEY DIJON, DJ

OC Introduces Patrik Ervell

Patrik Ervell moved seamlessly into fashion design after studying political science at UC Berkeley and then moving to New York to work as an editor at *V Magazine*. In 2005, Patrik launched his first full menswear collection at Opening Ceremony, already demonstrating his trademark precision, perfect white dress shirts, slim-fit tailoring, and Scandanavian knitwear. Horsehair braiding, recycled parachute jackets, and rubber coats have all won Patrik a reputation as an innovator, but he's never lost his reserved cool. No matter how unusual the materials, Patrik's designs are always firmly grounded in modern American sportswear classics. With his new line of womenswear, Patrik brings his trademark minimalist perfection to the girls that have been shopping his men's line all these years.

Every year when we do the CFDA/*Vogue* Fashion Fund, we see two to three designers that are new to us or just recently on our radar. But then you find out that they've been a part of Opening Ceremony, and have been on Opening Ceremony's radar for years. I think there's something really telling in that!

STEVEN KOLB, CHIEF EXECUTIVE OFFICER, CFDA

'05 UK

LEFT TO RIGHT: Patrik Ervell SS11, FW11, and FW12, all photographed for Opening Ceremony. RIGHT PAGE: Cloak clothing store on Greene Street, illustration by Benjamin Kress. FOLLOWING TWO SPREADS: Opening Ceremony SS05, photographed by Isabel Asha Penzlien; Opening Ceremony FW05, photographed by Isabel Asha Penzlien.

We opened a store for Cloak around the corner from OCNY.

When Opening Ceremony decided to expand its retail concept to open boutiques for other labels, cult menswear line Cloak was a logical choice. Working closely with Cloak designer Alexandre Plokhov to create a bespoke space in a tiny shop on Greene Street, Opening Ceremony extended its empire over lower SoHo. With its slim suits and restrained designs evoking the British mod era, Cloak was the go-to brand for a certain type of downtown man, who was welcomed by an antiqued *fumoir* vibe, rich wood paneling and a dressing room hidden behind a library wall. From 2005–2008, the legion Cloak fans had their New York clubhouse.

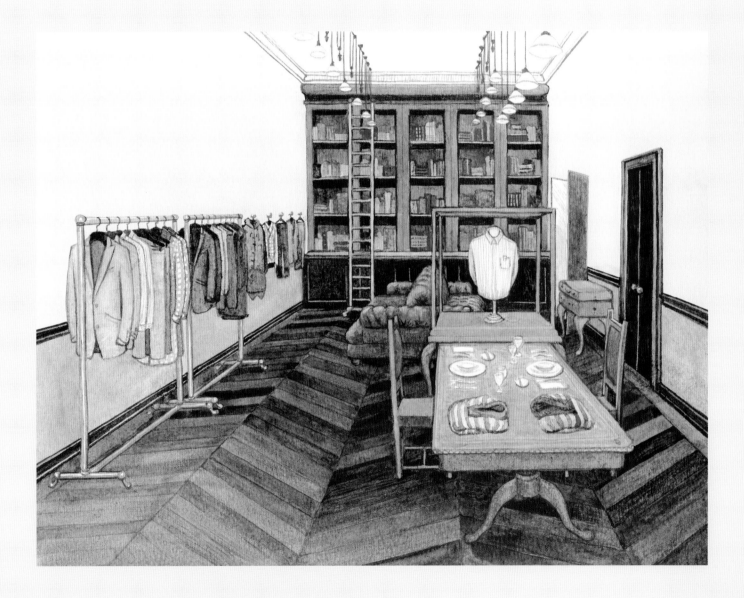

I worked with Humberto on the design of the Greene Street space. I wanted it to look like an English library. He found some amazing people from Brooklyn who built us this library shelving with a secret door. The whole collaboration was brilliant—it was the perfect space and concept for that time.

ALEXANDRE PLOKHOV, FASHION DESIGNER

Opening Ceremony introduced a new generation of international designers. They brought uptown women downtown to buy into new, high-end fashion. I think Opening Ceremony definitely created a new, conceptual way of buying into young designers and a lifestyle that has since flourished and become synonymous with the store.

MARIOS SCHWAB, FASHION DESIGNER

there is an opening ceremony and....
we all start the same,
cells grow to use cell fones ,
some form cells ,
some get put in cells ,
sex sells ,
greed breeds
and plants seeds
but we use new keys
to type
old deeds
set up by
old needs
but what do u read?
what was in ur feed
what is ur tv feed?
wheres ur internet lead?

things change and
change can have a range
but systems
shouldnt operate
by stickin zombies in a cage
i still dont do beige
but still do rage
for the simple fact
coz im still engaged
if i wasnt so fashion
i'd be a sage
so i fashion abLY
do cou rage
in the age of wage

OC × M.I.A.

The revolutionary British/Sri Lankan musician M.I.A. has continually touched the Opening Ceremony universe, starting with the fateful moment in 2005 when Humberto met her at local bar Max Fish while she was in town to promote her first sensational album, *Arular*. Humberto gave her a special necklace that he had brought back from Brazil, and a lasting bond was born. In 2008, M.I.A. sold Oakley Run, her limited-edition line of super-bright, body-conscious clothing, exclusively at Opening Ceremony. And in 2010, OC partnered with the incendiary performer for the launch party of her third album, *Maya*, at PS1 in Long Island City. As the artwork she made for the event attests, Opening Ceremony and M.I.A. have continued to share a self-reliant, independent, and curious approach to creativity.

CLOCKWISE FROM TOP RIGHT: Humberto and M.I.A. at Max Fish, 2005; M.I.A. performing at PS1 for the launch of *Maya* with Opening Ceremony, 2010; M.I.A.'s collection, Oakley Run, photographed for Opening Ceremony. LEFT PAGE: Artwork by M.I.A. for Opening Ceremony, 2011.

SWEDEN

Acne shop on Greene Street photographed by Michael Vahrenwald, 2012.

Jonny Johansson and Mikael Schiller with Carol and Humberto on 2006

Opening Ceremony and Sweden's Acne Studios have a close history: Opening Ceremony opened the first stateside Acne store on Greene Street. Carol had first discovered the brand on a 2004 trip to Berlin, which led to several visits to Stockholm and the decision to feature Swedish fashion in 2006. Acne (Ambition to Create Novel Expressions) was founded in 1996 by Jonny Johansson and three partners, as a collective that produced fashion, including their now classic denim line, alongside design, film production, and advertising work. Acne Studios is now a global force, with highly acclaimed ready-to-wear collections and the much-loved Acne Paper *magazine. Carol and Humberto met with Jonny and Mikael Schiller, Acne's executive chairman, in the Opening Ceremony office to discuss the personal affinity that helped to bring Swedish fashion to America.*

HUMBERTO: We wanted to feature Sweden in 2006 in part because of Acne. Carol had seen the collection on a trip to Germany, and we didn't know a lot of Swedish brands at the time. She came back home and said that we had to feature Sweden.

JONNY: Wow! That's cool.

HUMBERTO: A lot of people told us that 2006 was a launching point for Swedish fashion. It's amazing because our focus on the country really did start with Acne.

JONNY: That's really interesting because it shows how sensitive you guys are to what is going on. I wonder how you do it—I would like to have that in my DNA.

HUMBERTO: I feel like we go with our gut, and if it's something we're really excited about, we really go after it.

JONNY: That's very bold. You don't compromise on fashion, you sort of live it.

MIKAEL: Our jeans were quite popular from 2004 to 2006, but I think what we really appreciated about you was that you weren't really that into jeans! You kind of liked them, but for you it was the ready-to-wear collection that really stood out.

HUMBERTO: Carol and I had strict rules about Opening Ceremony not carrying denim. Everyone carries denim, and when that happens you become indebted to denim. Jonny, from your perspective, what was Swedish fashion like at that time? What made it an interesting moment to tap into?

JONNY: At that time everything was multidisciplinary and the creative world was loosening up. We could do a t-shirt line and sell it in a high-end store—we were able to crisscross within creative worlds. I think that was something we took on, and it was inspiring for the kids in Stockholm.

HUMBERTO: From our point of view, there was definitely an aesthetic that was Scandinavian. It felt like it was about reinventing basics, reinventing shapes, and allowing things to make sense that generally don't make sense together.

CAROL: There were a lot of parallels between our two companies: Acne was multi-faceted, with *Acne Paper*, graphic design, film production, and other elements. I also think Sweden was starting to have an outside influence at that time. This tiny country became a massive force in music, design, and fashion. When we visited Stockholm in 2006, the entire scene felt very alive. We saw The Magic Numbers play on one trip. We've always been into Swedish music such as Robyn, Neneh Cherry, Lykke Li....

MIKAEL: It's true. There's this fashion establishment [in Sweden] with these companies that have been around forever. What was refreshing about working with you is that you had a bit of the same background of, "Let's try it, let's do it!"

HUMBERTO: I've always felt like there was a naïveté. We weren't always burdened by expertise and that allows you to be free. We like to work with people we respect and admire, and they often come from different fields. That's the crux of it. ◆

109

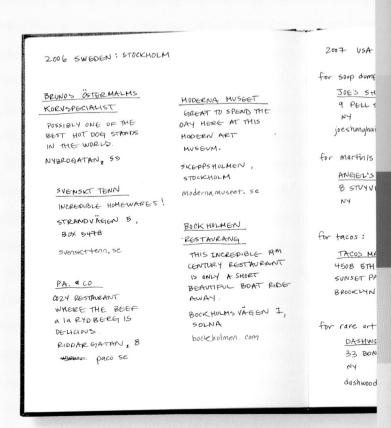

OC Introduces Acne

The Opening Ceremony team first visited Acne Studios' Stockholm headquarters in 2006, when Acne was still a slightly kooky creative collective running on a do-it-yourself, do-it-all basis. This struck a chord, and soon Acne's pieces were flying off the shelves of the New York shop. Eight years later, Acne is an international design phenomenon, a go-to denim brand, and Opening Ceremony's retail partner, with their own store just blocks away on Greene Street.

Jonny Johansson started Acne with three friends in the 90s, with the hopes of building something more than a fashion label. Though it was their modern, grungy clothing that took off first, Jonny and his friends have since put their hands in everything from manufacturing furniture to publishing their own in-house magazine, *Acne Paper*. Every branch of the Acne family taps into an instinctive sense of quirky, Scandinavian-cool that makes it greater than the sum of all its many, many parts.

CLOCKWISE FROM TOP LEFT: Jordan Robin in Acne FW11; Jordan Robin and Daniel Chew wearing the Acne x *Candy Magazine* collaboration line, photographed for Opening Ceremony, 2011; Acne shop. **FOLLOWING PAGE:** Acne jeans photographed by Zoë Ghertner, 2011.

OC Introduces Swedish Designers

The Swedish fashion scene in 2006 was characterized by functional, affordable, and refreshing sportswear for men and women. Brands like Ann-Sofie Back, Whyred, Velour, and Cheap Monday were all concerned with the creation of clothing that blended seamlessly into an urban landscape. Humberto and Carol made several trips to Sweden in 2005 and 2006, and were super excited by the discovery of fashion that was casual without being dowdy, and experimental without being outlandish.

Whyred, founded in 1999 by good friends Roland Hjort, Lena Patriksson Keller, and Jonas Clason, is a self-dubbed "indie super-label." Equally influenced by the big city, art, music, and good tailoring, Whyred's separates are the sort of intelligently luxurious pieces that can be worn every single day.

Velour has mastered the art of slim-cut, slightly preppy men's classics. Per Andersson began designing his line in 2002, after several years at the helm of one of Göteborg's most beloved clothing and design shops, Nostalgi. With a hint of the Swedish west coast maritime style, Velour pieces are contemporary standards.

A pioneer of experimental yet neutral basics, Ann-Sofie Back studied at Stockholm's Beckmans College of Art and Design and then Central Saint Martins in London. Ann-Sofie stayed in London after earning her master's in 1998, launched her eponymous line in 2001, and then began her secondary line, Back, in 2005. She returned to Stockholm in 2009 to serve as creative director of hometown favorite Cheap Monday.

At about fifty dollars a pop, Cheap Monday jeans were just about the cheapest, skinniest jeans around in 2006, and Opening Ceremony was the go-to destination to find them. As the epitome of affordable mid-2000s Swedish fashion, these jeans were worn by all the cool kids from St. Marks Place to Shibuya to Camden Lock. Now with full menswear and womenswear lines under the creative direction of Ann-Sofie Back, Cheap Monday has moved above and beyond the denim craze.

'06 SE

Opening Ceremony was one of the first shops that featured Swedish design, and now you can find it everywhere: Australia, Germany, Italy, China, Japan…. Being Swedish, it's kind of a weird concept, but it was obviously successful since it's been copied so much.

ANN-SOFIE BACK

LEFT: Cheap Monday photographed for Opening Ceremony; RIGHT: Opening Ceremony New York store during the year of Sweden, 2006. RIGHT PAGE, LEFT TO RIGHT: Whyred SS08, photographed by Andreas Sjödin; Ann-Sofie Back SS11, photographed by Stefan Zschernitz; Velour FW08, photographed by Per Zennström. FOLLOWING SPREAD: Opening Ceremony SS06, photo collages by Matt Keegan.

Opening Ceremony is the only store in New York that taps into a group of young designers that every other store might have been scared to touch. It is a place to find creative talent, inventive items, and off-the-grid labels.

SARAH MOONVES, STYLIST, SENIOR FASHION EDITOR,
T, THE NEW YORK TIMES STYLE MAGAZINE

Dan Colen created one of his iconic "Kiss" paintings especially for this book. Dan is one of the new guard of downtown New York artists, and is closely associated with Nate Lowman and fellow 2006 Whitney Biennial artist, the late Dash Snow. For two weeks in November 2011, Opening Ceremony friends, family, and customers kissed a piece of paper installed in the doorway of the flagship store in New York City. As a testament to the community of the store, customers and OC staff got intimate with the piece as it became saturated with multicolored kisses.

Dan Colen photographed by Terry Richardson, 2011. LEFT PAGE: "Kiss" painting by Dan Colen for Opening Ceremony, 2011.

CALIFORNIA

REPUBLIC

LOS ANGELES

Alexander Wang
photographed by Terry
Richardson, 2011.

Alexander Wang with Carol and Humberto on 2007

The astronomical rise of fashion designer Alexander Wang is inseparable from his New York neighbors, Opening Ceremony. Just a few years ago, Alex was a Parsons student browsing at the store, and now he is one of its most treasured designers, with a shop-in-shop at Opening Ceremony Los Angeles, and a deep section at all locations. Since its inception in 2005 as a small knitwear line, the Alexander Wang brand has gone from a sleekly cool insider secret to a worldwide, CFDA/ Vogue Fashion Fund winning phenomenon, with its bags and shoes gracing the coolest girls' wish lists. Carol and Humberto walked down the street to Alex's Chinatown headquarters to discuss the parallel evolutions of their businesses, Opening Ceremony's New York vs. Los Angeles year, and their mutual Asian food fixations.

CAROL: 2007 was a big year for both of us. That's the year you started your line and we opened our Los Angeles store.

HUMBERTO: We would always see you shopping in the store even before that, when you were a student at Parsons.

ALEXANDER: I did! I just thought the concept was really unique, that every year it changed themes in terms of the country that it represented. You guys really started the whole movement in the Howard Street/Crosby Street area, before Jil Sander and Derek Lam were there. And I love the LA store— there's always kind of a sense of discovery; you never know what's right around the corner. I remember when you guys first told me that it used to be Charlie Chaplin's dance studio and I thought it was so cool.

HUMBERTO: It was totally abandoned and kind of spooky when we found it.

CAROL: We remember going to buy your first collection. How old were you then?

ALEXANDER: I was 23! The most exciting thing about Opening Ceremony for us at the beginning was that you bought heavily into our runway pieces. Humberto, when you come into the showroom, you pull aside, like, five pieces on a rack. Usually, that's the selection for someone's entire store. But for you, those are the only pieces you *don't* take. It was always great to have that partnership and for someone to believe in us.

CAROL: Do you remember when we opened the Alexander Wang shop-in-shop in LA?

ALEXANDER: Yes! We did that little party for it. That was a really fun night, because we had M.I.A. host it. What I loved is that Humberto said, "What should we do for the catering, should we do a dinner?" And I was like, "I've always wanted to try your mom's cooking." You said, "Well, my mom's available!" So Wendy did the cooking. It was great! She did an amazing job. I just love the atmosphere that you guys have created for your team—it's sort of like an extended family. Alexander Wang is a family business, too, with a similar culture. Also, with you two, I've always had the kind of relationship where it's one step closer than what I have with normal buyers. We're Chinatown neighbors, so we talk about local Asian restaurants. We'll always chat: "Do you know this Vietnamese sandwich place in this weird little mall off Mulberry Street?"

CAROL: Asian food is key! We're all native Californians in New York, and while LA is not a different country, it sometimes feels like it! A lot of people say your brand is very New York, but I see some elements of Cali in it.

ALEXANDER: In the beginning you reference certain things, and since New York was new for me at the time I was excited by a lot of the references I saw, so immediately it was translated into my work. And just like how Opening Ceremony is a global brand now, we're a global brand, too. So now I really see our vision as something global. In terms of the California aspect, I've always had a sense of ease in my approach—and a sense of taking the pretentiousness out of fashion. I think that's something I've always loved about Opening Ceremony, as well, that when you walk into the store it's always a very friendly environment. Maybe that has something to do with the fact that we're all from California, where it's about not taking anything so seriously, where it's about having fun. Fashion is just a way for people to express themselves—it's not life or death.

CAROL: Another big thing we did in 2007 was launch the Proenza Schouler for Target line in the store. For us, that was a clear indicator of this kind of high/low moment in fashion, which got really exciting. It was validating for us because we've always liked mixing runway pieces with t-shirts and random souvenirs. I think your line has always been about mixing luxury and streetwear, too.

ALEXANDER: What I love is that when I go to Opening Ceremony you're not just buying clothes—Opening Ceremony is a lifestyle. I go there and I buy things beyond clothing, like the toner that I can't get anywhere else except for in ▶

Paris. When we started Alexander Wang, it was never about being "contemporary" or being "designer," we were just like, "We're going to create things we love, and our girls can wear t-shirts and leather parkas, and it's okay for it to all fall into different price categories but live under one roof." We don't believe that value is measured by a price tag—that just because something is expensive means it's validated. And I think that's a new way of approaching fashion, and that's why we feel so connected to Opening Ceremony. It's not a traditional department store, it's a new outlook.

HUMBERTO: In a way, you're a new type of fashion brand that was only able to develop in the 2000s and Opening Ceremony is a new kind of store that was only able to develop in the 2000s.

ALEXANDER: Yes. We grew up together! ◆

We expanded our world westward, opening a Los Angeles store!

Opening Ceremony is like a huge, continual piece of fabric.
Everyone who collaborates with them does so with such
respect and intention for what we're all stitching together.

ERIN WASSON, MODEL, ACTRESS, AND DESIGNER

OC staff and friends at
Opening Ceremony Los
Angeles, photographed by
Isabel Asha Penzlien for
i-D magazine, 2007. LEFT
PAGE: Opening Ceremony
Los Angeles photographed
by Isabel Asha Penzlien.
FOLLOWING SPREAD:
Opening Ceremony Los
Angeles photographed by
Michael Vahrenwald, 2012.

OCLA is in Charlie Chaplin's former dance studio!

In 2007, Opening Ceremony opened its Los Angeles store, just off Melrose Boulevard in West Hollywood. Located in Charlie Chaplin's former dance studio, the 10,000-square-foot space was inspired by the Southern California mall culture of Carol and Humberto's adolescence. With a sprawling space designed to evoke the surrounding freeways, Opening Ceremony LA captures the laid-back and distinctively Cali vibe of its founders' home state.

With a hint of the nostalgia for our suburban youth, we opened a mini-mall at OCLA.

Opening Ceremony LA's second-floor mini-mall concept takes Carol and Humberto's "teenage dream mall" concept one step further, with shop-in shops offering a rotating cast of brands that has included Acne, Nom de Guerre, Mayle, Topshop, Exquisite Costume, Schiesser Revival, D.A.P., Other Music, Boy. by Band of Outsiders, Band of Outsiders, and Alexander Wang. Creating unique environments for each brand's personality, but still under the Opening Ceremony umbrella, the mini-mall brings a constellation of friends and partners to the Los Angeles store.

'07 CA

A few years ago, Opening Ceremony approached me about doing a pop-up bookstore in their Los Angeles location. As Carol and Humberto selected the kinds of books they wanted to carry, it became clear just how important art and culture are to them. Fashion companies associating with the art world have become, at best, a cliché. But in the world of Opening Ceremony, art is part of life. The artist whose book they carry is likely a friend, and look—they're wearing Opening Ceremony!

ALEXANDER GALAN, VICE PRESIDENT, ARTBOOK | D.A.P.

The Little House of Accessories joined our LA store...

The Little House of Accessories is exactly what its name evokes: a cute little cabin that displays all of the bits and baubles that call Opening Ceremony home. Exclusive to this Los Angeles location is Carrie Imberman's selection of estate jewelry, sourced from her family's legendary Kentshire boutiques in New York.

We are a seventy-year-old family business specializing in antique and estate jewelry and furniture, with a decidedly old-school clientele. Perhaps an unlikely fit for OC. However, when I approached Humberto and Carol with the idea that I'd like to curate a capsule collection of vintage fine and costume jewelry for a more fashion-oriented audience, their attitude was, "Of course, how obvious! Let's do it— fun!" The next thing I knew, we were quickly ensconced in their LA store, with Humberto's mom even designing and installing a chic Opening Ceremony logo window grate within six hours after I bitched about security.

CARRIE IMBERMAN, VICE PRESIDENT, KENTSHIRE

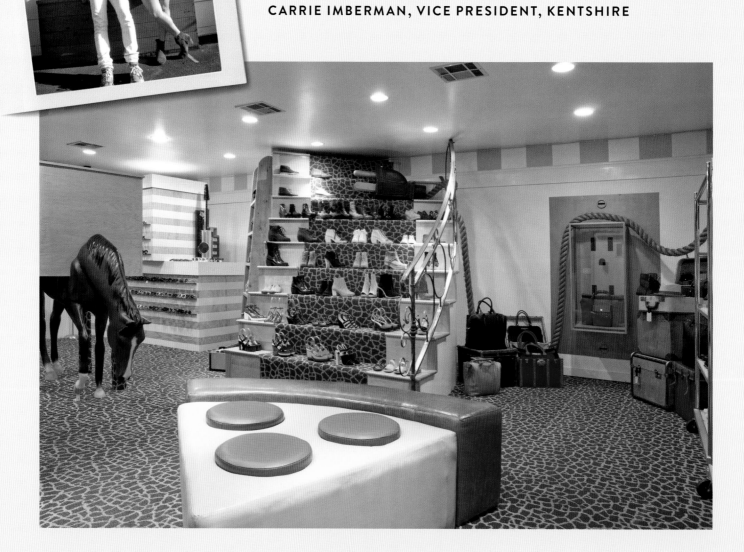

...and we commissioned Spike Jonze to do an installation of air balloons!

Because a new parking lot is potentially boring but giant anthropomorphic balloons are definitely *not*, Opening Ceremony commissioned Spike Jonze to make a site-specific installation for the official opening of the store's Los Angeles parking lot: giant blow-up balloons he dubbed "You and Me." Inspired by the bobbing balloons that dot car dealerships throughout Los Angeles, the piece was recorded for posterity in a short film by Gia Coppola, *You and Me on La Cienega*.

129

Sketches and images of Spike Jonze's "You and Me" installation. LEFT PAGE, TOP: Carol and Humberto in front of the Little House of Accessories; BELOW: Little House of Accessories, photographed by Michael Vahrenwald, 2012. PREVIOUS SPREAD, TOP LEFT: Band of Outsiders lego installation photographed by Scott Sternberg. ALL OTHER IMAGES: Opening Ceremony Los Angeles mini-mall photographed by Michael Vahrenwald, 2012.

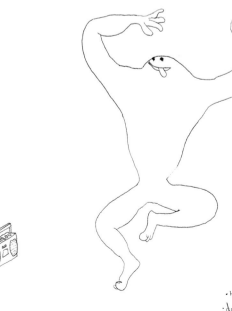

OC Introduces Alexander Wang...

Whether it was handing out fortune cookies at our 2009 Fashion's Night Out event, creating an exclusive men's denim collection for the New York store, or simply showing up to every Opening Ceremony party with the biggest posse of models, Alexander Wang has been inextricable from Opening Ceremony's story.

Before the celebrity name-checks, sold out collections, CFDA/*Vogue* Fashion Fund award, and of course, his greatly anticipated runway shows, Alexander Wang would visit Opening Ceremony's New York store between his classes at Parsons. After creating a small knitwear capsule line in 2005, Alexander launched his first full women's collection in 2007, when he was only 23 years old. Today, Alexander Wang has expanded his label to include ready-to-wear, eveningwear, loungewear, the T by Alexander Wang collection, sunglasses, footwear, and accessories.

Excited by Wang's refreshing and thoroughly downtown take on what girls wanted to wear, Carol and Humberto began to buy deep into his vision every season. In 2009, Opening Ceremony created the ongoing Alexander Wang shop-in-shop at the Los Angeles location. His classic t-shirts are standbys for the store's buyers, and the team sits front row at his shows twice each year. Most importantly, one can still bump into him at local Chinatown noodle joints.

'07 CA

Band of Outsiders...

Former Hollywood agent Scott Sternberg created Band of Outsiders in 2004, combining the perfect amounts of prep and cool. With a sartorial commitment to simple items such as blazers and oxford shirts, he is always trying to make the basics even better. He's won himself a pretty rabid following, including the actors that grace his Polaroid lookbooks.

Many former Band of Outsiders interns have gone on to work at Opening Ceremony, a phenomenon documented in Scott's Opening Ceremony blog column, *The Band of Outsiders Intern Files*. In 2007, Band of Outsiders and LEGO built a shop-in-shop at the Los Angeles store, and for the 2009 Fashion's Night Out festivities, Scott combined his two loves, fashion and cookies, at his Band of Outsiders and Momofuku Milk Bar cookie stand. Now an Opening Ceremony staple, the Los Angeles brand has grown to include womenswear lines: Boy. by Band of Outsiders, and the more feminine Girl by Band of Outsiders.

...and Jeremy Scott

Since 1997, Beverly Hills-based Jeremy Scott has been putting the fun into fashion. With an almost-obsessive eye for pop culture, his collections are always laced with a healthy dose of humor. Whether he is showing in Paris, New York, or Los Angeles, there is always a snap-worthy group of starlets and club kids in the audience of his shows. What other designer could find inspiration in *The Flintstones* and 90s raves, or make an ironic cameo in Larry Clark's film *Wassup Rockers*?

In 2007, Carol and Humberto first brought Jeremy's designs into the stores, where they don't sit long before selling out. The next year, Jeremy began designing with sportswear stalwart Adidas, creating playful items such as teddy bear high-top sneakers, a tasselled tank, and a matador-inspired sweatshirt. Jeremy's recent and ongoing collaborations with sunglasses specialist Linda Farrow and timekeepers Swatch prove that Jeremy's wild, enviable sense of color and imagination know no bounds.

131

Jeremy Scott x Adidas Originals SS09 and FW09, photographed for Opening Ceremony. **LEFT PAGE, TOP:** Alexander Wang SS10, photographed for Opening Ceremony; **BOTTOM:** Jason Schwartzman for Band of Outsiders FW09, Kirsten Dunst for Boy. by Band of Outsiders SS11, photographed by Scott Sternberg.

Our events are family affairs, with dinners cooked by Humberto's mom!

Alexander Wang launched his line of sunglasses for Linda Farrow with the dinner to end all dinners at Opening Ceremony Los Angeles. Humberto's mama, Wendy Leon, prepared a twelve-course feast, including Peking duck and winter melon soup, for guests including M.I.A., Jason Schwartzman, and Chloë Sevigny.

ALEX, ME, CHLOË & CAROL

OUR FRIEND THE TABLE

'07 CA

COOL. WENDY!

JASON, CHESTNUT HAIR, & BRIAN

CAROL & BRADY

ME & CLAIRE

Regardless if its address is in Manhattan or Tokyo, or a virtual address on the web, visiting Opening Ceremony is an immersive experience. It's almost like a parallel universe, where the best things are at once high and low, expensive and cheap, with elements that somehow elevate one another and live in this unique place. Humberto and Carol really are genius curators, and continue to define the taste of this generation.

STEFANO TONCHI, EDITOR-IN-CHIEF, *W* MAGAZINE

TOP: Stefano Tonchi photographed by Terry Richardson, 2011; BOTTOM INSET: Stills from OCTV's "Show and Tell with Stefano Tonchi," 2011. LEFT PAGE: All Polaroids by Carol and Humberto.

OC × Proenza Schouler for Target

We launched Proenza Schouler's collection for Target at the store.

Before mass-market collaborations became de rigueur, Jack McCollough and Lazaro Hernandez of Proenza Schouler designed an instantly acclaimed and adored line for Target's GO International Designer Collective. As friends, it felt natural to launch the collection at Opening Ceremony, with a shopping event and bash at the New York store. Shoppers snapped up pieces including palm-printed party dresses and brightly colored bustier tops.

'07 CA

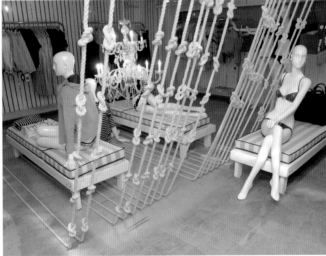

It's difficult to imagine so many young designers, such as Proenza Schouler, being as successful without Opening Ceremony. I don't know of another retailer that invests in them and allows them to express themselves the way Opening Ceremony does.

SIMON COLLINS, DEAN, SCHOOL OF FASHION, PARSONS THE NEW SCHOOL FOR DESIGN

In-store merchandising for Proenza Schouler for Target. LEFT PAGE, TOP: Lazaro Hernandez, Amy Astley, Jack McCollough; BOTTOM: Proenza Schouler for Target launch party at Opening Ceremony New York. FOLLOWING TWO SPREADS: Opening Ceremony SS07, photographed by Isabel Asha Penzlien.

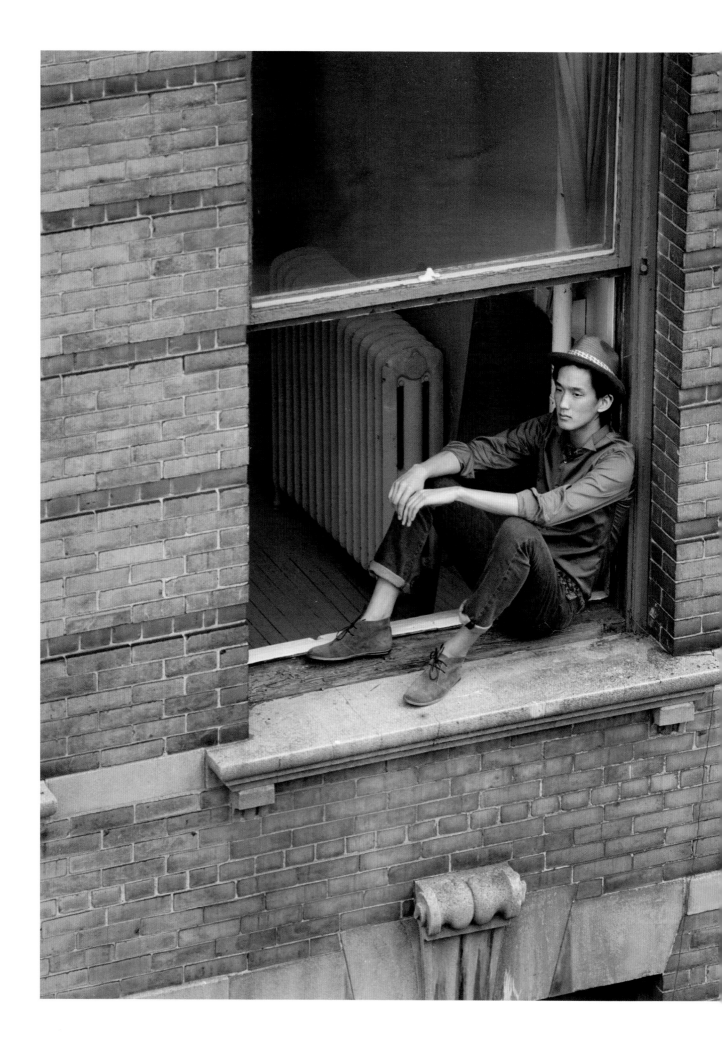

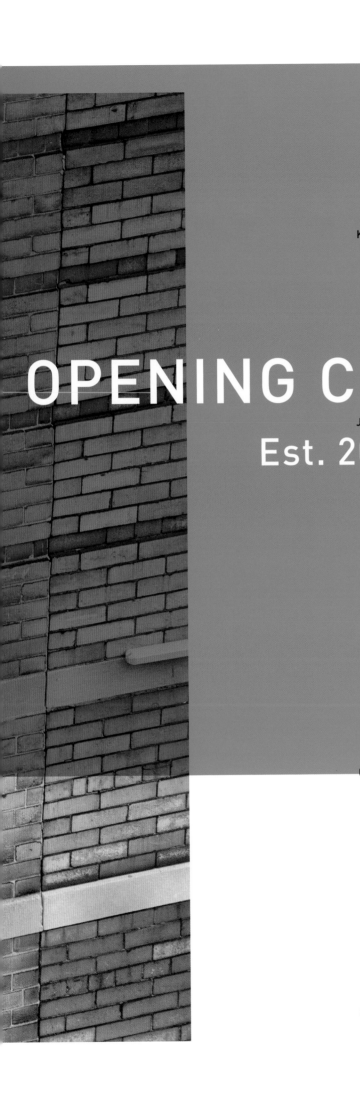

OPENING CEREMONY
Est. 2002

BRAZIL
Alexandre Herchcovitch
Amapo
Dieego
Maxime Perelmuter
Melissa
Neon

GERMANY
Bernhard Willhelm Shoes
Bless
Kostas Murkudis for Schiesser
Lutz
Pulver
Schiesser Revival
Vera and Daphne Correll

GREAT BRITAIN
And I
AND by Judy Blame
Back by Ann-Sofie Back
Barbour
B Store
F-Troupe
Gareth Pugh
Hussein Chalayan
Jessica Ogden for Fred Perry
Judy Blame
Kim Jones
Marios Schwab
Peter Jensen
Richard Nicoll
Swear
Topshop
Topman
Umbro by Kim Jones

SWEDEN
Acne Jeans
Bea Szenfeld
Burfitt
Carin Wester
Cheap Monday
Diana Orving
Fifth Avenue Shoe Repair
Hope
Minimarket
Nakkna
Pour
Rodebjer
Ulrika Sandstrom
Velour
Whyred

UNITED STATES OF AMERICA
Band of Outsiders
Benjamin Cho
Cloak
Crumley
Driftwood
Elizabeth Yarborough
Gerard Tully
Hansel from Basel
Josh Hickey
Kendi
Loden Dager
Mary Ping
Miki Tanaka
Opening Ceremony
Patrik Ervell
Proenza Schouler
Rachel Comey
Risto Bimbiloski
Slow & Steady Wins the Race
thorn
United Bamboo

2008

JAPAN

Derek Blasberg
photographed by Terry
Richardson, 2011.

Derek Blasberg with Carol and Humberto on 2008

The New York Times has called him the Truman Capote of his generation, but to Opening Ceremony, the writer Derek Blasberg is an old friend who reliably enlivens fashion shows and parties. Derek serves as Senior Editor of V Magazine *and* V Man *and is also editor-at-large at* Harper's Bazaar. *He has recently had a slew of success with his cheeky bestselling book* Classy: Exceptional Advice for the Extremely Modern Lady *and its sequel* Very Classy: Even More Exceptional Advice for the Extremely Modern Lady. *Carol and Humberto spoke with Derek over a transatlantic call that was full of dish, memories, and a bit of hard-earned fashion wisdom.*

DEREK: Let's talk about 2008.

CAROL: It was a huge year for us because of the Olympics in Beijing, so we did all these events and partnerships. We kept the store open for 72 hours during the Olympic Opening Ceremony.

DEREK: I remember that! I loved that party. Who doesn't love a three-day retail rave? I came in the wee hours.

HUMBERTO: Yes, I can remember you coming in at three in the morning with a bunch of girls!

DEREK: It's a genius idea to promote shopping while intoxicated—one that I can really get behind. Another great idea from that same year was your collaboration with Chloë Sevigny. I love that lady as much as you guys do. Did you know that it was going to be such a big partnership?

HUMBERTO: No way. She was at a party and someone asked her if she would ever do her own collection, and she said, "never." But the one thing she would do is design a few dresses for Opening Ceremony. I read it in *Women's Wear Daily.*

DEREK: And then you just called her up?

HUMBERTO: Yep. It's amazing that it turned into a full collection that has lasted this long. The rule was, and still is, that she would have to want to wear everything. She's really making clothes she loves, and of the collaborations we've done, the Chloë collection is one of the most natural.

DEREK: You guys were friends before the collaboration, right?

HUMBERTO: She would shop at the store and we would always go to Morrissey night at Sway together, but we've become much better friends now. Making the collection together has been a really intimate experience—we've learned a lot about each other in the last four years.

DEREK: Three words for you: Leopard print cardigan.

CAROL: Oh no! You and that cardigan.

DEREK: Yes, in Chloë's first men's collection she made a leopard print cardigan that I absolutely loved. I saw it in the store one day and thought I would come back the following day to buy it. But when I came back, it was gone. Gone! I called the other stores, and no one could find it for me. This cardigan haunts me in my sleep, guys.

CAROL: OK, we'll tell her. Maybe she can do a special reissue.

DEREK: If I'm going to be honest here, I'll have to admit that some of my Opening Ceremony memories are a little hazy. Especially all the parties that you've done, that's when it gets a little foggy.

CAROL: We love having you at our parties.

HUMBERTO: We've done some together, haven't we?

DEREK: Yes, and we've done them all over the place: New York, Paris…. What I think is so great about an OC party is that it's such a mix of people. It's all over the place: uptown, downtown, hip, young, old, rich, and poor. There are all these legitimately cool people mixed in with people who think they're really cool, which is the category I probably fall into.

CAROL: What's so great is that you've been there since the beginning.

HUMBERTO: We were friends even before we opened the shop.

DEREK: From a financial point of view, it's been great to see things evolve from this cute little downtown shop to—no joke—a major fashion industry powerhouse. You have your own shows now, stores all over the world, diffusion lines, and you're even taking over French luxury brands. I just can't believe it's been ten years. On the one hand, it feels like it's only been ten minutes, but on the other, you guys have accomplished so much. It's almost depressing to see how much you've done.

CAROL: Now, Derek, don't sell yourself short—you're a best selling author and you work with amazing people every day! You've done a few things, too.

DEREK: Wait! I just had another Opening Ceremony flashback: Carol, do you remember when I found you in the 26th Street garage flea market, trolling the racks for old Pendleton Baja jackets? Wasn't that around 2008?

CAROL: Yes! That's when the seeds for our Pendleton collaboration were being planted, and we were doing research. You were looking at this jacket, and I remember that as soon as you put it down I snapped it up and bought it.

DEREK: Another fashion regret. I should have gotten that jacket!

HUMBERTO: But if you had bought that jacket our Pendleton ▶

collaboration might not have ever happened.

DEREK: You're right. You see? I'm a giver. You're welcome, Carol and Humberto.

CAROL: Now that I think about it, we probably should have sent you one of the jackets as a thank-you gift.

DEREK: Don't be silly. You've already given me so much. Just by being friends with you guys, my cool points have gone up. I like that: cooler by association. In fact, that should be the Opening Ceremony tagline: "Making kids cooler, one leopard print cardigan at a time." ◆

'08 JP

2008   JAPAN : TOKYO

TOKYU HANDS
YOU CAN FIND
EVERYTHING AT THIS
AMAZING MULTI-LEVEL
STORE. WE LOVE
THE STICKERS!

12-18 UDAGAWA-CHO,
SHIBUYA-KU

tokyu-hands.co.jp/en

CHIPAO MARATAN
YOU CAN PICK YOUR
OWN INGREDIENTS &
HAVE THEM MAKE
A CUSTOM NOODLE
SOUP FOR YOU!

15-18 SAKURAGAOKA
SHIBUYA

maratan.com

COW BOOKS
OUT OF PRINT BOOKS.
1-14-11 AOBADAI,
NAKAMEGURO,
MEGURO-KU

cowbooks.jp

KIMUKATSU
THE BEST TONKATSU
YOU WILL EVER TRY.

4-9-5 EBISU,
SHIBUYA-KU

MOS BURGER
REALLY HITS
THE SPOT AFTER A
LATE NIGHT OF
OOLONG HI'S.

all over town!

TABIO
THE BEST SOCKS!
AND YOU CAN
EMBROIDER YOUR
INITIALS.

B2F OMOTESANDO
HILLS MAIN BLDG
2-10 JINGUMAE,
SHIBUYA-KU

tabio.com

TOP: Opening Ceremony team members Jacky Tang and Sachiko Murayama in Tokyo; BOTTOM: Opening Ceremony team in Tokyo. RIGHT PAGE: Carol in Tokyo.

We always eat our way through the countries we visit, from dim sum to shabu-shabu!

When I was working with Carol and Humberto on opening the Japan store, there were so many late nights and so many late night snacks. I learned that Carol and Humberto really love food, and approach it with the same passion as they have for fashion. Conveyor belt sushi, Japanese pastas, udon, ramen, soba, kima katsu, okonomiyaki house parties, MOS Burger vs. Freshness Burger, beef bowls, and rice balls. Like a small party or a shopping spree adventure, they're always up for a snack.

SEAN LINEZO, "PROFESSOR BEAR"

OC Introduces N. Hoolywood...

As a young buyer, Daisuke Obana earned the nickname Mister Hollywood when he would travel to Los Angeles just to buy vintage clothing. It was this love of vintage that inspired Daisuke to create N. Hoolywood, one of Japan's most popular menswear lines and a true cult brand. N. Hoolywood joined the Opening Ceremony Showroom in 2008, introducing the brand to the US market.

Like most ingenious Japanese designers, it is Daisuke's eye for peculiar detailing, paired with exemplary menswear cuts, that sets him above most. N. Hoolywood's line includes outerwear, suiting, shirts, underwear, and even socks. Daisuke now shows in New York, and hops between the east and west coasts and his native Japan, still collecting authentic American vintage pieces to inspire his work.

'08 JP

Tsumori Chisato...

Cats, cartoons, and crayon colors: Tsumori Chisato's world is a magical enclave of childlike delight and imagination. Putting on hold her girlhood dream to become a manga illustrator, Tsumori studied at Tokyo's esteemed Bunka Fashion College before beginning her career as a designer at Issey Miyake Sport in 1977. With the support of Mr. Miyake himself, Tsumori launched her own line in 1990. Longtime fans of the brand, Humberto and Carol were excited to bring Tsumori into the fold for Opening Ceremony's year of Japan.

Tsumori Chisato now has flagship stores in both Tokyo and Paris, and although she has strong ties to both countries, her real talent lies in the otherworldly realm of her own imagination. Tsumori's free-flowing silks and hand-drawn illustrations and prints have won her a band of loyal followers enchanted by her spectral magic.

Toga...

Designer Yasuko Furuta founded Tokyo-based label Toga in 1997, three years after graduating from Paris' ESMOD. Since then, her unique formula for whimsical, multi-layered dressing has won her credit with the critics and a legion of fans. Draped neon silks, patterned stockings, and schoolgirl collars pair with punky, deconstructed silhouettes to land Toga's aesthetic in a domain of its own.

With a family of secondary lines that now encompasses vintage, menswear, and the younger Toga Pulla collection, Toga's empire is only getting bigger. At its center, the flagship store in Tokyo's Harajuku district has become a mecca for cult fashion in the heartland of cult. Filled floor-to-ceiling with Yasuko's colorful prints and vintage finds, it's the perfect embodiment of Toga's unique vision.

...and Suno

When fashion designer Erin Beatty and filmmaker Max Osterweis launched Suno in 2008, their old San Francisco friends Carol and Humberto were first in line for the preview. Not only did they buy the entire collection, but Suno became an Opening Ceremony Showroom brand shortly thereafter. The fabrics for the first collection were taken from Max's collection of vintage Kenyan kanga textiles acquired during years of vacationing on Lamu Island, and each piece was one of a kind and numbered, in addition to being produced with equitable labour in Western Africa.

Suno has since advanced its initial concept, with Max and Erin traveling year-round to India, Peru, and, always, Africa to source ethical and indigenous ways of creating beautiful clothing. Whether working with traditional Andean embroidery or Sub-Saharan madras, the pair has created a totally international brand that speaks the local language.

147

Suno SS11, FW11, and SS11, all photographed for Opening Ceremony. LEFT PAGE, TOP: N. Hoolywood SS11, photographed by Katsuhide Morimoto; CENTER: Tsumori Chisato Resort '12 and SS11, photographed for Opening Ceremony; BOTTOM: Toga SS11, photographed by Chikashi Suzuki.

On August 8, 2008, we commemorated the Beijing Olympics opening ceremony with a 72-hour extravaganza!

For the occasion of the opening ceremony of the 2008 Beijing Olympics, Opening Ceremony kept its New York store open for 72 hours straight on August 8, 2008, with activities and sports-related shenanigans galore. Hercules and Love Affair performed at the store, Saved Tattoo founder Scott Campbell inked Olympic tattoos, Astrology Zone's Susan Miller gave astrological readings, jewelry designer Philip Crangi hosted a ping pong tournament, and *MTV* host SuChin Pak was the MC for a Championship Scrabble competition. A special collaboration with Nike included gold and silver Air Max 1 sneakers and limited-edition posters and t-shirts celebrating the games.

'08 JP

Merchandising and festivity snapshots from the 8-8-08 celebration at Opening Ceremony New York.

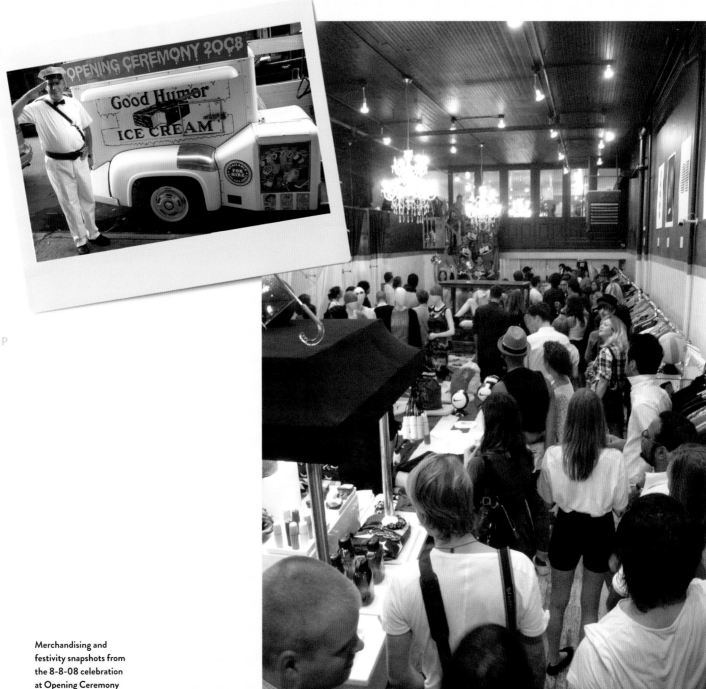

Over the years we have made hundreds of seriously kawaii trinkets for our stores.

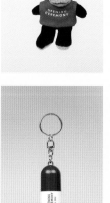

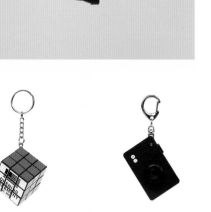

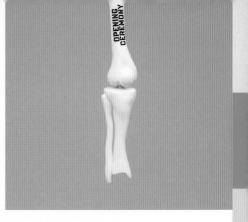

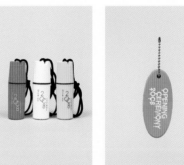

ConfettiSystem has made some awesome decorations for our stores and events.

Opening Ceremony and art-party masters ConfettiSystem share a shredded and sparkly history. Nicholas Andersen and Julie Ho make beautifully-hued tissue paper creations, including piñatas, garlands, and made-to-order floral set pieces. The pair have brought the party everywhere, from United Bamboo's spring 2009 campaign with Terence Koh to Beach House's world tour, plus a music video for Beyoncé and custom décor for Lanvin. For Opening Ceremony, ConfettiSystem created a Cinco de Mayo window display for the 2009 Rodarte collection, designed giant suitcases and travel elements for Opening Ceremony's 2011 Target event at the Ace Hotel, and created the giant, otherworldly heads on many of the store's mannequins.

'08 JP

ConfettiSystem store window display for Rodarte SS09. LEFT PAGE: ConfettiSystem store window displays at Opening Ceremony New York and OC at Ace Hotel locations, 2009–2011. FOLLOWING SPREAD: Opening Ceremony SS08, photographed by Isabel Asha Penzlien. PAGES 156–159: Opening Ceremony FW08, photographed by KT Auleta, illustrations by Ippy Patterson.

OPENING CEREMONY

Est. 2002

35 Howard Street, New York
451 North La Cienega Boulevard, Los Angeles

CHLOË SEVIGNY FOR OPENING CEREMONY

CLOCKWISE FROM TOP LEFT: Slits show, LA, photograph by Lizzi Bougatsos, 2009; Photograph by Harmony Korine, 1997; Hydra, Greece, photograph by Tara Subkoff, 2004; Weed Beach, CT, photograph by Chloë's mom, 1984; Morrissey show, Miami, photograph by Patrick O'Dell; Photograph by Slater Bradley, 1994. FRONT COVER: Photograph by Terry Richardson, 2011.

Chloë Stevens Sevigny

i'd like to dedicate my small portion
of this bigger picture to. su. gay.
jesse and nicole. candy darling
and the color pink. leopard and
liberty prints. the irregular regulars
redheads, and pin ups. s & m,
skater boys, and rebel girls.
robert mapplethorpe. clunky shoes,
caffine and paisley. polka dots.
houndstooth, gapped teeth, and
teen dreams. tomboys and dandies.
dave gahan, eyelets and corsets.
the slits, delinquents, duellists.
and renegades. and above all,
carol and humberto

xxx ccc.

CHLOË SEVIGNY for OPENING CEREMONY
SPRING SUMMER 2008
photographed by Mark Borthwick.

For her first collection in collaboration with Opening
Ceremony, actress and style icon Chloë Sevigny tapped
into the Liberty floral prints and gingham of her
preppy Connecticut childhood, and paired them with
the form-fitting styles of the 80s and 90s. Made
to be worn by Chloë and her friends, the collection
featured Chloë's personal wardrobe basics, including
black booties and swingy skirts. For the debut, Chloë
curated a special flipbook featuring all the looks
in the collection, with photography shot by Mark
Borthwick, remixed with drawings by Rita Ackermann,
Dan Colen, Spencer Sweeney, and Amy Gartrell.

Chloë Sevigny for Opening Ceremony
flipbook, SS08, photographed
by Mark Borthwick. Artwork by
Marika Thunder (BOTTOM LEFT),
Lizzi Bougatsos (BOTTOM RIGHT),
and Amy Gartrell (LEFT PAGE).
PREVIOUS SPREAD: SS08 flipbook.

PHOTOGRAPHY
KT AULETA
STYLING
BENJAMIN STURGILL

DRESS AND BOOTS CHLOE SEVIGNY FOR
OPENING CEREMONY S/S
SOCKS THE SOCKMAN

POLO

CLOCKWISE FROM TOP: In-store
display; Chloë, Humberto, and
friends after the presentation;
Humberto and Max Farago; Invitation
to the Chloë Sevigny for Opening
Ceremony x ~~Self Service~~ magazine x
MAC event at Webster Hall.
LEFT PAGE: Chloë photographed by
KT Auleta for ~~V~~ magazine, 2008.

For the fall of 2009, Chloë launched a
completely unisex collection, reinterpreting
menswear classics for both men and women. A few
Chloë insta-classics were born this season,
notably the multi-strap buckle wedge and the
baggy leopard-print cardigan. Chloë staged a
presentation of her friends modeling the looks
at London Fashion Week, and worked with David
Armstrong to produce a limited-edition book of
redheads wearing her collection, called Reds.

CHLOË SEVIGNY FOR OPENING CEREMONY

CLOCKWISE FROM TOP LEFT: Maryam
L'Ange, Chloë, and Lissy Trullie
photographed by Lele Saveri;
Chloë; Chloë Sevigny for Opening
Ceremony FW09 presentation in London
photographed by Lele Saveri. LEFT
PAGE, CLOCKWISE FROM TOP LEFT:
Jesse Hudnutt; Lissy Trullie;
Louise Benson; Maryam L'Ange
photographed by Marcio Madeira.

Images from *Reds* by David Armstrong, made with Chloë Sevigny for Opening Ceremony, FW09.

Chloë and friends photographed by KT Auleta for *Vogue Homme Japan*, FW09.

PJ Ransone
俳優

★シャツ ¥38,850　★パンツ
¥51,450　サスペンダー（参考商品）
★シューズ ¥24,150／すべてChloe
Sevigny for Opening Ceremony
（オープニングセレモニープレスルーム）

Jesse Hudnutt
オープニング セレモニースタッフ

ジャケット ¥101,850　ベルト
¥12,600　パンツ ¥50,400　★シュ
ーズ ¥24,150／すべてChloe
Sevigny for Opening Ceremony
（オープニングセレモニープレスルーム）

Tony
アーティスト、スケーター

★ニット ¥31,500　シャツ ¥38,850
パンツ ¥51,450　★シューズ
¥25,200／すべてChloe Sevigny
for Opening Ceremony（オープニ
ングセレモニープレスルーム）

Chloë Sevigny
女優、デザイナー

コート ¥24,950　シャツ ¥38,850
バッグ（参考商品）　シューズ
¥68,250／すべてChloe Sevigny
for Opening Ceremony（オープニ
ングセレモニープレスルーム）

Hair: Jeff Francis at The Wall Group
Makeup: Fabiola Arancibia at The Wall Group
Photo assistants: Jordan Seiler and Nyra Lang
Digital Capture: Joe Gunn

My Favorite Boyfriends

NYから届いたスペシャル・プレゼント！

NY、ロウワーイーストサイドを歩くクロエ・セヴィニーと6人の男たち。
クロエがお気に入りのボーイフレンドたちのためにデザインした
クロエ セヴィニー フォー オープニング セレモニーを、
ヴォーグ オム ジャパンの読者にスペシャル・プレゼントします。
あなたもクロエのボーイフレンドになりませんか？

Photography **KT Auleta** | Styling **Chloë Sevigny**

M.Blash
映像作家

ニット ¥47,250　パンツ ¥36,750　★
シューズ ¥25,200／すべてCHLOË
SEVIGNY FOR OPENING
CEREMONY（オープニングセレモ
ニープレスルーム）

Humberto Leon
オープニングセレモニーオーナー

ニット ¥50,400　★シャツ ¥38,850
★シューズ ¥24,150／すべて
CHLOË SEVIGNY FOR
OPENING CEREMONY（オープ
ニングセレモニープレスルーム）

Joe DeNardo
アーティスト

ジャケット（参考商品）　★バッグ
¥38,850　パンツ¥50,400　シューズ
¥54,600／すべてCHLOË
SEVIGNY FOR OPENING
CEREMONY（オープニングセレモ
ニープレスルーム）

★印の商品はプレゼントとなります。洋服はMサイズ、シューズは27cm（アメリカサイズ9）をご用意しています。応募方法はp.197-198をご参照ください。

I love the idea of Chloë looking over New York, because it's her town.

KT Auleta, photographer

Chloë Sevigny for Opening
Ceremony supports the Robert
Mapplethorpe Foundation.

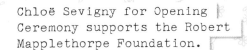

Chloë Sevigny for Opening
Ceremony t-shirts supporting
the Robert Mapplethorpe
Foundation. LEFT PAGE AND
PREVIOUS SPREAD: Chloë Sevigny
for Opening Ceremony Resort '11,
photographed by KT Auleta.

For her first resort collection with Opening
Ceremony, Chloë played with repetition and
recombination by producing five dresses named
after her best girl friends, each dress available
in five different prints. Presented at a garden
party at the Elizabeth Street sculpture garden,
the collection was a lighthearted, delightful
offering, which included special t-shirts in
support of the Robert Mapplethorpe Foundation.

Chloë Sevigny for Opening Ceremony
Resort '11 Garden Party. CLOCKWISE
FROM TOP LEFT: Lesley Arfin; Carol
Lim; Blue Sorrenti; Anna Gray.
RIGHT PAGE: Lissy Trullie, Chloë
Sevigny, and Lizzi Bougatsos.

CHLOË SEVIGNY for OPENING CEREMONY
RESORT 2012
photographed by Tim Barber.

Chloë Sevigny for Opening Ceremony runway, Resort '12, photographed by Maria Valentino. RIGHT PAGE, CLOCKWISE FROM TOP: Runway setup; Runway show; Sketch by Chloë; Humberto, Chloë, and Carol, photographed by Greg Kessler.

In the summer of 2011, Chloë staged her first ever official runway show with Opening Ceremony for her Resort 2012 collection. Presented in a NoLita gymnasium, and featuring an art installation by Charles Wing, the show had models, including Jenny Shimizu and Christina Kruse, donning looks focused on provocative leather and innocent eyelet. Chloë also paired with legendary skate brand Vision Street Wear on a co-branded capsule collection.

Runway and backstage
images photographed
by Greg Kessler and
Opening Ceremony.

opening
ceremony
press

PARTNERSHIPS

'09 ×

Terence Koh with Carol and Humberto on 2009

Born in Beijing and raised in Canada, Terence Koh is one of his generation's most lauded artists, and a true original whose delicate monastic manner and pure white wardrobe are inimitable. His multimedia work and performance pieces have been included in countless group and solo exhibitions, including the 2004 Whitney Biennial, an eponymous solo exhibition at the Whitney Museum in 2007, and a mid-career retrospective titled "Love for Eternity" at MUSAC in Leon, Spain in 2008. Even better, until closing in 2011, Terence's Asia Song Society gallery was Opening Ceremony's neighbor and a Chinatown fixture. His cult zine Asian Punk Boy *was sold at Opening Ceremony, and he collaborated with the company in 2009 on a capsule collection called* The Whole Family. *Carol and Humberto sat with him in a darkened room of his lofty apartment, as he served water in white teacups.*

CAROL: One of the things that has been really interesting is revisiting everything that has happened in the New York art scene in parallel to the store. In 2009, the year of Opening Ceremony partnerships, we collaborated with you on The Whole Family collection. We wanted to focus on celebrating all the people we love working with. But even before that we were neighbors, and your gallery, Asia Song Society, was right down the block. I remember you bringing your parents to the store as early as 2002—I feel like you've seen it grow from the beginning.

TERENCE: I remember you guys both working in the back of the store. You were even sewing stuff yourselves; I remember there was a sewing machine. We felt a part of it.

HUMBERTO: It is still a meeting place for a lot of people.

TERENCE: Like a market place! It's very organic, don't you think? The progression of it is.

HUMBERTO: Yes. The creative family is something OC really stands for. That's why The Whole Family was so perfect. Where did that concept first come from?

TERENCE: It was the title of my first show. It was called "The Whole Family" because it was with all kinds of family, between my real family and my family of friends. But it was also a play on the word "whole" because there are bullet holes in the t-shirts. And I remember I really wanted a tag that said "bullet" on it. I like making little tags.

HUMBERTO: Geographically, we've always felt close to you. There have always been a lot of artists and designers around the Canal Street/Chinatown area.

TERENCE: In 2009, Chinatown was more like a secret spot.

Not so secret anymore.

HUMBERTO: It's less of a secret now.

TERENCE: A friend of mine is always saying we should be sentimental about New York, but not too sentimental. Howard Street used to be dirtier—there was all this garbage, more Chinese restaurants, and more rats. Even today it's kind of secret. You have to almost know Howard Street, even though it's off Broadway.

CAROL: That's true.

TERENCE: It kind of nestles.

HUMBERTO: But now you've moved a bit uptown?

TERENCE: Yes. I'm excited about my new studio. We're trying out a boy and a girl as my main helpers because I believe in this yin-yang thing, about this energy of male and female. I want them to wear a uniform. For the girl, I think it's going to be a really simple white skirt with a round button. For the guy, a nice white sweater with a round button and pants. But I want something that's really comfortable so that when they're working it's like they're almost in pajamas, in Santa's little workshop. The idea is that when you come into the studio, you take off your worldly outfits. I almost want a shelf where you put your wallet and your cell phone. It's almost like being a monk as you cast off your worldly possessions. I really love that idea.

CAROL: I want to come to Koh World.

HUMBERTO: Do you think that Carol and I have a yin-yang balance in our partnership?

TERENCE: Definitely. I see you guys playing off each other when deciding what to buy for the store. I can see you guys having this conversation, like a debate. And I think it definitely helps—instead of it being a kind of single vision, again, it makes it like a family vision. At the Opening Ceremony store, I know the girls go to the men's section, but I have a feeling that men are not limited to going to the men's section. Do you think that works?

CAROL: Definitely.

HUMBERTO: We don't think that it is gender-specific. Carol and I are very insistent that the store has both men's and women's in every part, so that you kind of travel together to every floor, and there isn't a strict line between the two. We like that there's a little bit of a gray area.

TERENCE: So Japan was featured in 2008, 2009 was partnerships, and 2010 was France?

HUMBERTO: Yes.

TERENCE: So 2009 was between Japan and France. Japanese and French...2009 could almost be Vietnamese. [*Laughs*] ◆

OC × Terence Koh

Quintessential New York artist Terence Koh created a collection for Opening Ceremony called The Whole Family in fall of 2009. Already renowned within the art world for his mystical all-white performances, our friend and neighbor easily became one of our most iconic collaborators. With printed t-shirts featuring the slogan THE WHOLE FAMILY, as well as a pearl-encrusted shirt, Terence brought his distinctively eerie monochromatic universe to Howard Street. For its window, Terence created a white neon sign spelling out THE WHOLE FAMILY, which now graces the wall of the Opening Ceremony office.

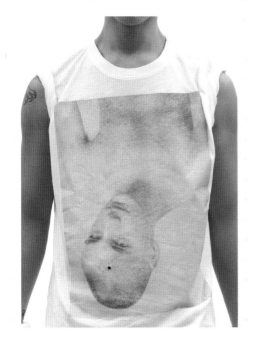

CLOCKWISE FROM TOP: Terence Koh and Humberto in front of Terence's window installation at Opening Ceremony New York; Pearl-encrusted t-shirt, Terence Koh for Opening Ceremony; Terence Koh x Opening Ceremony x Forfex shoes; Terence Koh for Opening Ceremony t-shirts. **LEFT PAGE:** Drawing by Terence Koh for Opening Ceremony, 2011.

OC × Pendleton

Opening Ceremony began a lasting and impactful partnership with classic American heritage brand Pendleton in fall '09. Carol and Humberto remembered Kurt Cobain's Pendleton flannels, which reminded them of growing up with the outdoor side of the brand in California. Bridging the traditional flannel and wool prints of the Oregon brand with a more modern sensibility, the men's and women's collections were an immediate hit that brought the institution back to life, setting a precedent for a wave of Americana nostalgia in fashion.

'09 ×

CLOCKWISE FROM TOP LEFT: Pendleton meets Opening Ceremony clothing tag; SS10 photographed by Christelle De Castro; FW10 photographed by Kathy Lo. **RIGHT PAGE:** SS10 photographed by Christelle De Castro. **FOLLOWING TWO SPREADS:** FW09 photographed by Richard Kern; SS11 photographed by Christelle De Castro.

We are inspired by every country we visit, including America!

We have been a family business, making and weaving cloth for six generations, since 1863. One of the things about working with Opening Ceremony is that we can see its family atmosphere. And it's really a good feeling that our family and the Opening Ceremony family share some of the same values. Opening Ceremony inspired us to look differently at who we are; they gave us confidence to reach out to a new consumer.

MORT BISHOP III, PRESIDENT, PENDLETON WOOLEN MILLS

Opening Ceremony team at the Pendleton Round-Up rodeo, 2011.
RIGHT PAGE, CLOCKWISE FROM TOP LEFT: Opening Ceremony & Timberland hang tag; Convenience Boot, FW09; Water Shoe, SS11; Pendleton Meets Opening Ceremony x Timberland Roll Top Boot, FW10; Boot Oxford, SS12; Boot Oxford, SS12; Water Shoe, SS10; 7-eye boot, FW09; Water Shoe, SS10, all photographed for Opening Ceremony.

OC × Timberland

Timberland and Opening Ceremony share an ongoing partnership, which began in 2009. The idea for the collaboration was born when Humberto spotted a dapper dude wearing a pair of the brand's classic laced 6-inch boots, and shortly thereafter Humberto unearthed a pair of rare moccasin-soled lug boots in Japan. In 2010, Opening Ceremony reissued the classic water shoes, with new colorways that were an instant sensation. New twists on other classic Timberland silhouettes are part of the 2012 season: the lug sole boat shoe and boot oxford work shoe. Opening Ceremony's first three-way collaboration was a synergistic boot made in collaboration with Pendleton and Timberland. It featured Native American jacquard wool on a classic fold-down boot style.

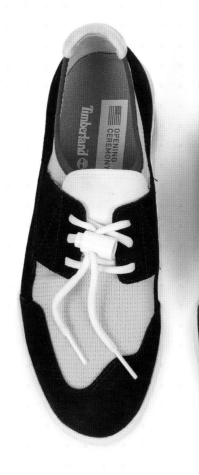

Opening Ceremony was the first brand
in a long, long time that really appreciated
and saw value in my archives.

BETSEY JOHNSON

Betsey Johnson
photographed by Terry
Richardson, 2011.

OC × Betsey Johnson

For the 30th anniversary of Betsey Johnson's label, the legendary New York designer partnered with Opening Ceremony to produce a collection of her classic archived looks. What New York 80s and 90s girl does not remember buying little Betsey dresses? Pulling from her eponymous label, as well as her first mass retail lines, Alley Cat and Paraphernalia, the pieces ran the gamut of Johnson's history, featuring sugary-sexy classics including cherry prints, peplum skirts, textured black mini dresses, and lace-up fastenings.

TOP: Betsey Johnson Archive curated by Opening Ceremony lookbook FW09, photographed by Sebastian Kim; BOTTOM: Betsey Johnson and Humberto.

BETSEY + HL

OC × Dr. Martens

Humberto bought his first pair of Dr. Martens in 1991 to wear to the inaugural Lollapalooza festival, a purchase that launched an enduring obsession and collection that lasts to this day. The first Dr. Martens for Opening Ceremony collaborative collection was inspired by Humberto's original 8-hole Docs, based on the since-discontinued 1980s shoe silhouette that he considers the perfect combination of chunky and streamlined. The first Dr. Martens for Opening Ceremony shoes were released in 2010, just in time for Dr. Martens' 50th anniversary celebration. A subsequent collection expanded to include the high-heeled Darcie boot and the Lily sandal in a variety of plush animal prints.

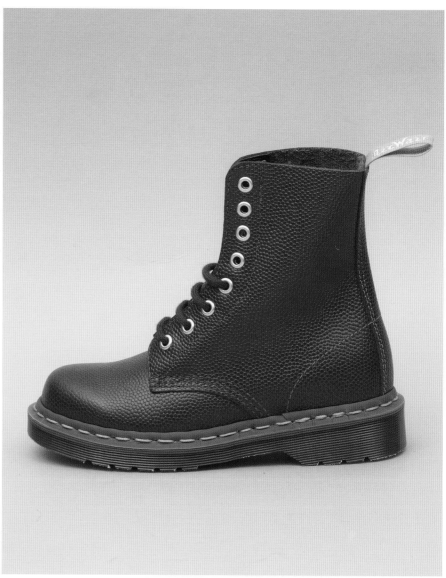

'09 ×

CLOCKWISE FROM TOP LEFT: Dr. Martens for Opening Ceremony 1461 shoe, FW10; 8-eye boot, FW11; Lily Velcro sandal, SS10; Lily Velcro sandal, SS10; Darcie boot, SS10, all photographed for Opening Ceremony.

OC × Gitman Brothers

Opening Ceremony teamed up with classic American shirtmaker Gitman Brothers to produce a collection of fine men's shirts and basics, with a distinctively Opening Ceremony flavor. Founded in 1978, Gitman Brothers is a proudly Made-in-USA brand that boasts rigorously constructed shirting. Humberto had the idea to update the shirts with a slimmer fit and to incorporate patterns such as tiny American flags and leopard print (as seen on rapper Drake). For the launch of Opening Ceremony Japan, Opening Ceremony created a limited-edition collection of multicolor dip-dyed Gitman shirts.

Gitman Brothers Expressly for Opening Ceremony, SS11, FW11, and SS12, photographed for Opening Ceremony.

Max Suit photographed
by Reid Ulrich, concept
by Samantha Sussman.
RIGHT PAGE, CLOCKWISE
FROM TOP: Catherine
Keener and Wendy Leon;
Clothing tag; Spike Jonze
at Opening Ceremony
Tokyo. FOLLOWING
SPREAD: Opening
Ceremony x Where
the Wild Things Are
collection, photographed
for Opening Ceremony.

OC × *Where the Wild Things Are*

Best buds Spike and Humberto jumped at the chance to collaborate with each other on a collection based on Spike's movie *Where the Wild Things Are*. Inspired by Spike's film adaptation of Maurice Sendak's much-loved book, the line featured a full range of faux fur pieces, evoking Max's crew of wild friends including Carol, Judith, K.W., Douglas, and Bull. The collection sold out in hours.

Spike [Jonze] and I went to visit Humberto at the store. Humberto's mom was there, too. They had such a beautiful window with the most amazing collection of *Wild Things*-inspired coats and jackets. We all started messing around, and I put on Max's wolf suit and jumped over to Humberto's mother to try to freak her out. She seemed amused, though pretty much unfazed. It made me wonder what Humberto must have been like growing up.

CATHERINE KEENER, ACTOR

WHERE THE WILD THINGS ARE

OPENING CEREMONY
Est. 2002

OC Introduces Pamela Love...

A native New Yorker with a background as an artist and stylist, Pamela Love began making jewelry in her Brooklyn basement in 2006. The eponymous Pamela Love line is now a highly coveted international brand, while her pieces remain handmade and personal. Love's awesomely organic work in metal synthesizes a deep relationship with the American Southwest, along with a fascination with astrology, nature, and the occult.

Love began selling her jewelry at the store in 2009, and that same year produced a collection for Opening Ceremony to celebrate the release of Spike Jonze's *Where the Wild Things Are*. Since then, her pieces including wildlife elements such as talons, crystals, and animals have become accessories integral to Opening Ceremony's environment.

'09 ×

Pamela Love jewelry photographed for Opening Ceremony. RIGHT PAGE: Jewelry by Delfina Delettrez photographed for Opening Ceremony.

...and Delfina Delettrez

Delfina Delettrez, a jewelry designer from the illustrious Fendi fashion family, launched her own line in 2007. Her whimsical pieces incorporate the natural and mythological worlds, using recurring imagery such as skulls, insects, flowers, lips, eyes, and religious artifacts. In recent years, her Paris Fashion Week presentations have become must-see events that might include anything from a moving conveyor belt based on a traditional Italian factory design to custom-made multicolored headwear from a wigmaker for the Roman opera. With pieces such as crystal pendants encasing tiny scissors and a bracelet in the shape of a black widow spider, Delfina challenges perceptions of costume jewelry by pairing the mystical with the mundane.

What I like about Carol and Humberto is that they give you blank paper, so you can be just as creative as you want.

DELFINA DELETTREZ

OC × Uniqlo

For Spring 2009, Opening Ceremony collaborated on a capsule collection of menswear for Japanese mass-market apparel brand Uniqlo. With a well-edited selection of slightly off-kilter classics for men, including blazers and button-downs, the collection was a runaway international hit.

'09 ×

Uniqlo x Opening Ceremony SS09, photographed for Opening Ceremony.
RIGHT PAGE: Sweaters by Jim Drain, photographed for Opening Ceremony.

OC × Jim Drain

New York artist Jim Drain collaborated with Opening Ceremony on a capsule collection of sweaters integrating the playfulness of his textile-based artwork with the wearability of ready-to-wear. Using an industrial knitting machine that he discovered while in undergrad at RISD, Jim created men's and women's sweaters with intensely colored, humorous, pixelated patterns. Known for his large-scale sculpture, which often incorporates hand-knit and fabric elements, Jim had long been one of Opening Ceremony's favorite artists. With prints inspired by found photographs, emoticons, and Atari video games, Jim made some of Opening Ceremony's all time favorite knits with a knowing wink.

When I met Carol and Humberto, I quickly learned that they loved the styling and quintessential American story of Keds. Humberto actually had collected rare vintage Keds from the USA and Japan. Opening Ceremony does a great job of creating a unique shopping experience, mixing vintage and modern and luxury and inexpensive goods in unexpected ways. In Keds' case, it means reinventing a classic—taking a brand and product that has held iconic status in American culture for 95 years and reinterpreting it for their audience.

TOM SLOSBERG, KEDS

Baseballs made for Fashion's Night Out, 2011, photographed by Zoë Ghertner. RIGHT PAGE, CLOCKWISE FROM TOP LEFT: French toile and striped sneakers, FW10; Keds at Opening Ceremony animal-printed sneakers, FW09; Keds at Opening Ceremony sneakers, Resort '12; bandana-printed sneakers, FW09, all photographed for Opening Ceremony. FOLLOWING TWO SPREADS: Opening Ceremony SS09, photographed by KT Auleta.

OC × Keds

In 2009, Opening Ceremony joined forces with the classic American sneaker
brand, creating an Americana collection that featured bandana print and
denim fabrics, followed by a Brit-punk series featuring neon and animal prints.
For Opening Ceremony's 2010 year of France, a Gallic line of Keds included
Toile de Jouy and striped incarnations, including a limited-edition shoe, hand-
embroidered by artist Richard Saja. In 2011, Opening Ceremony reissued the
much-loved ball-stitched baseball sneaker.

OPENING CEREMONY

Est. 2002

openingceremony.us

We opened an eight-floor, 50,000-square-foot department store in Tokyo!

Opening Ceremony opened its eight-floor, 50,000-square-foot store in Japan's Shibuya district on August 30, 2011, to huge fanfare. Inspired by the effusive shopping culture of Tokyo, Carol and Humberto wanted to create a department store done differently. Riffing off the mini-mall concept they had developed on the second floor of Opening Ceremony Los Angeles, Opening Ceremony Tokyo features shop-in-shops for Alexander Wang, Boy. by Band of Outsiders, D.A.P. books, Other Music, Trash & Vaudeville, and The Row. Each floor feels completely different, sampling American architectural and design styles such as 60s modernist, Santa Fe and southwestern craft, Victorian, and a typical American office setting. The opening bash was unforgettable, with The Strokes frontman Julian Casablancas performing, and a host of friends on hand, including Kirsten Dunst, Jason Schwartzman, Mary-Kate and Ashley Olsen, Erin Wasson, Alexander Wang, Rinko Kikuchi, and Yoko Ono, not to mention the extended Opening Ceremony family, friends, and staff.

'09 ×

CLOCKWISE FROM TOP LEFT: Humberto and Carol with the ceremonial sake table for the Opening Ceremony Tokyo grand opening; Mary-Kate Olsen and Ashley Olsen, Jason Schwartzman, and Rinko Kikuchi on the opening's red carpet, photographed by Takaryo (Eltio). RIGHT PAGE: Store views of Opening Ceremony Tokyo, photographed by Kozo Takayama. PREVIOUS TWO SPREADS: Opening Ceremony FW09, photographed by Richard Kern. FOLLOWING SPREAD: Opening Ceremony Tokyo exterior, photographed by Kozo Takayama.

Opening Ceremony lets me be what I want to be anytime and anywhere: casual, tough, sexy, whatever. Sometimes their clothes give you the answers, and sometimes they make suggestions.
RINKO KIKUCHI, ACTOR

OPENING CEREMONY

Est 2002

We always do Fashion's Night Out our way, with performances, limited-edition looks, and of course, delicious food!

Fashion's Night Out was developed in 2009 by Anna Wintour and *Vogue* as a "global fashion stimulus package" designed to kickstart retail. With shopping parties and special events in stores all over New York and internationally, Fashion's Night Out is designed to get shoppers excited about the fashion world in a truly democratic way. We have taken this template for Fashion's Night Out and run with it, outdoing ourselves every year with the most exciting event in New York, and Anna Wintour has consistently pointed to Opening Ceremony as exemplary of what can be achieved during Fashion's Night Out. In the first year, Opening Ceremony created a trunk show at Howard Street, complete with snacks from Momofuku Milk Bar and Van Leeuwen ice cream, and exclusive limited-edition designs from designers like Rodarte, Band of Outsiders, and Alexander Wang.

OPENING CEREMONY
HOWARD ST "TRUNK" SHOW
FNO 2009

'09 ×

TOP: Exterior of Opening Ceremony New York; BOTTOM: Fashion's Night Out merchandise, 2009–2011. RIGHT PAGE: Exterior of Opening Ceremony New York, photographed by Rebekah Miles.

'09 ×

Bonjour!
C'est mon genre de marché !

I thought for a long time that Carol and Humberto were a couple.

SARAH ANDELMAN, BUYER/ CREATIVE DIRECTOR, COLETTE

OPENING CEREMONY
MERCADO
DE CARNAVAL
FNO 2011

235

CLOCKWISE FROM TOP:
Jeffrey Steingarten hosting
a wine tasting; Terry
Richardson; *OCTV*'s "La
Videoteca," film of the
evening; Carol, Spike, Miss
Piggy, and Humberto; A
guest with cotton candy. All
photographs from Fashion's
Night Out, 2011. **LEFT
PAGE, CLOCKWISE FROM TOP:**
Opening Ceremony team
member Malik Winslow;
OCTV's "La Vidéotèque,"
film of the evening;
Humberto and Carol; a
Marie Antoinette model
with a pair of Keds. All
photographs from Fashion's
Night Out, 2010.

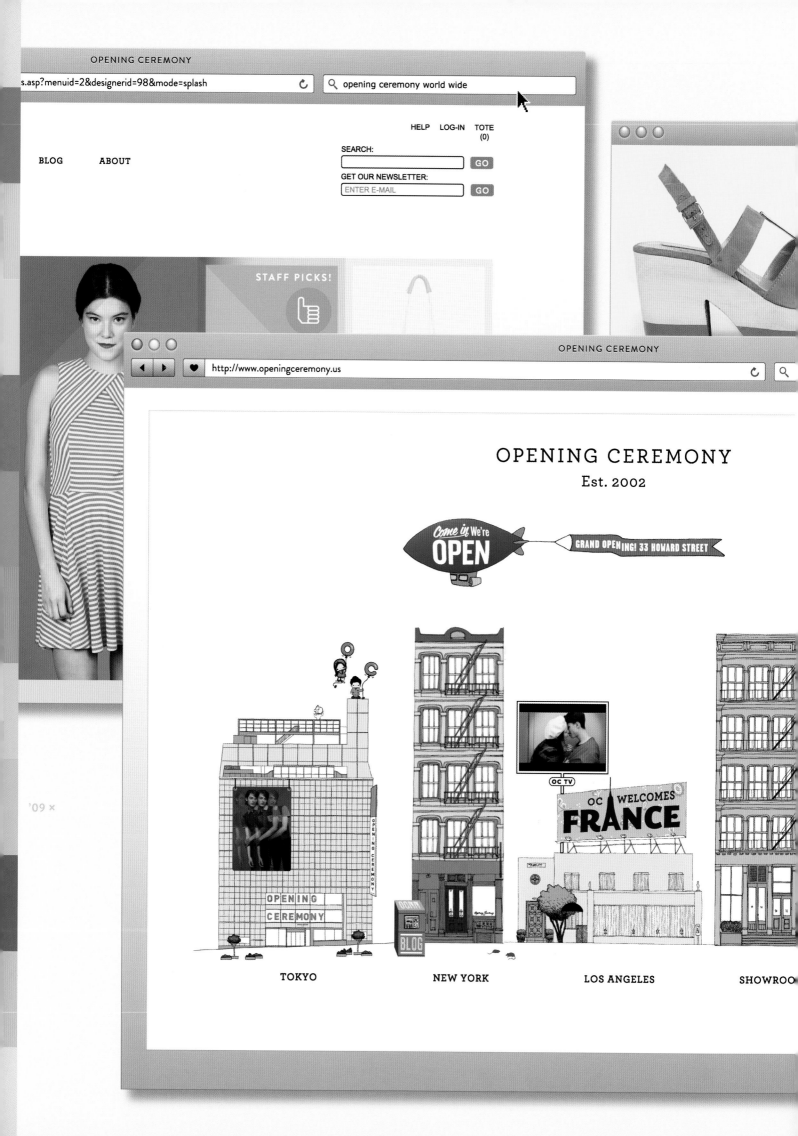

We brought our global community online!

Opening Ceremony Worldwide translates the stores' brick-and-mortar concept to an interactive multimedia shopping and content experience. With a devoted following around the world since its inception in 2009, the website features e-commerce with a distinctively personal twist, with friends and family serving as models and experimental editorials shot by photographers from Opening Ceremony's extended creative community. The "Opening Ceremony New News" blog has run interviews with everyone from Anna Wintour to Jean Paul Gaultier to Terence Koh, as well as still-life photography, event photos, and musings by contributors, including Chrissie Miller, JD Samson, Miranda July, Rob Pruitt, Ryan McGinley, and Lesley Arfin.

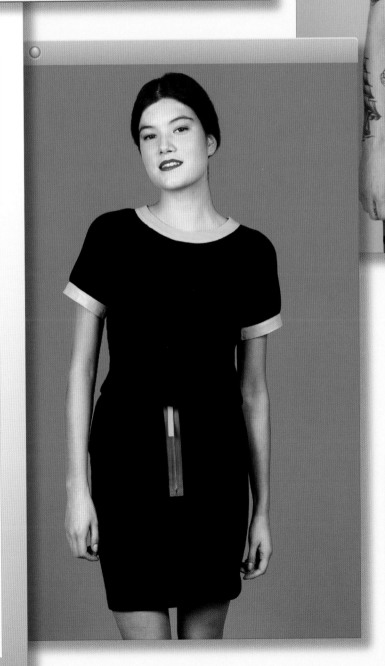

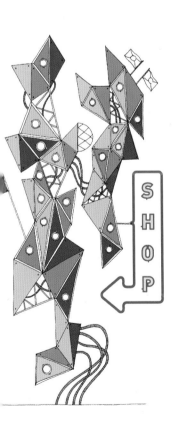

SHOP

WORLDWIDE

webphoto

su_archive

237

Opening Ceremony home-page illustrated by Alejandro Cardenas; All photography for Opening Ceremony. **FOLLOWING SPREAD, CLOCKWISE FROM TOP LEFT:** Hannelore Knuts gifs by Jason Oliver Goodman, FW11; Zippora Seven photographed by William Eadon, SS11; Delfina Delettrez photographed for Opening Ceremony; Kate Foley; Anna Wintour interviewed by Humberto on the Opening Ceremony blog, 2010.

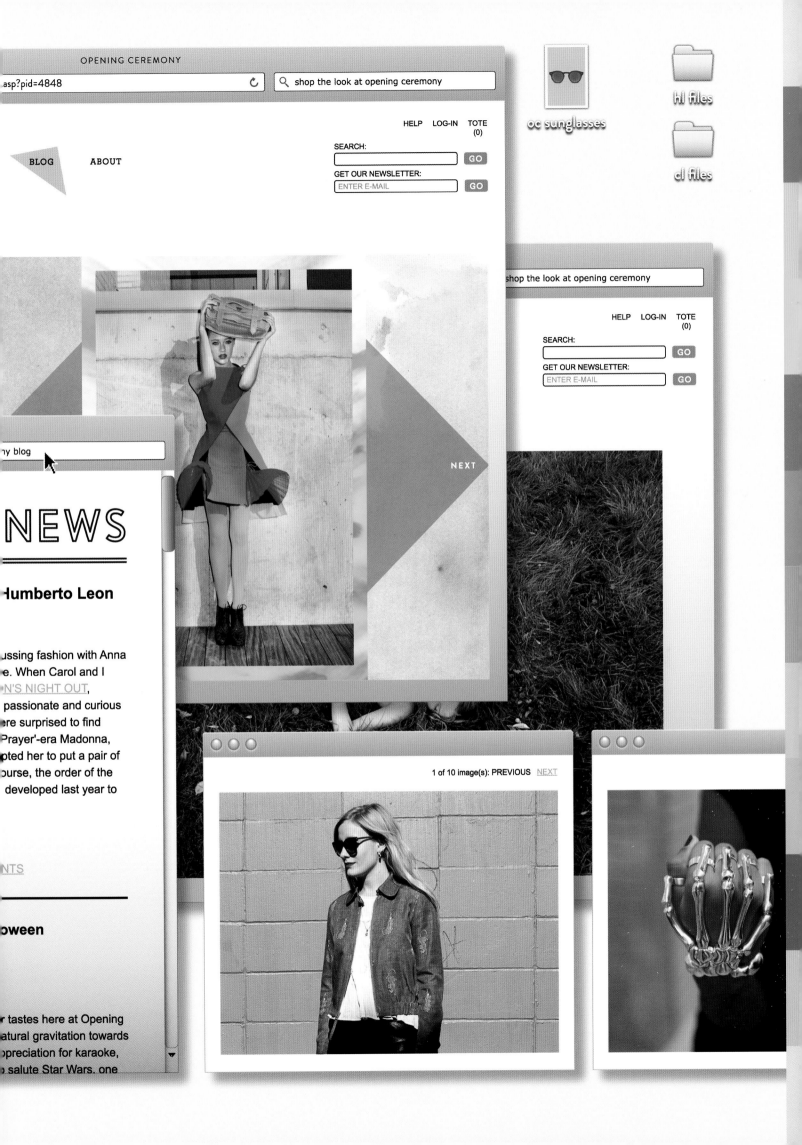

OPENING CEREMONY

...asp?pid=4848

shop the look at opening ceremony

HELP   LOG-IN   TOTE
(0)

SEARCH:

GO

GET OUR NEWSLETTER:

ENTER E-MAIL

GO

BLOG   ABOUT

oc sunglasses

hl files

cl files

shop the look at opening ceremony

HELP   LOG-IN   TOTE
(0)

SEARCH:

GO

GET OUR NEWSLETTER:

ENTER E-MAIL

GO

NEXT

...ny blog

NEWS

...Humberto Leon

...ussing fashion with Anna
...e. When Carol and I
...N'S NIGHT OUT,
...passionate and curious
...re surprised to find
...Prayer'-era Madonna,
...pted her to put a pair of
...ourse, the order of the
...developed last year to

...NTS

...oween

1 of 10 image(s): PREVIOUS   NEXT

...r tastes here at Opening
...atural gravitation towards
...preciation for karaoke,
...o salute Star Wars, one

André Saraiva
photographed by Terry
Richardson, 2011.

André Saraiva with Carol and Humberto on 2010

André Saraiva, the multi-hyphenate artist, invited Humberto and Carol to his airy white Chinatown studio to discuss classic Americana, the idea of a modern Renaissance, and Opening Ceremony's year of France. André's playful and colorful graffiti (particularly his "Love Graffiti" project of paramours' names) was already splashed around Paris and Tokyo before he opened Parisian standby clubs Le Baron and Le Montana, Le Baron's Tokyo outpost (and its forthcoming New York incarnation), as well as hotels in Paris and Saint-Tropez. Now, André has added creative director of L'Officiel Hommes *to his resume, but he still spends much of his day drawing with markers.*

HUMBERTO: 2010 was our year of France, and you're one of our closest French friends, so we wanted to get your take on how we represented the country.

ANDRÉ: It was visionary to feature France that year. French people were taking more of an interest in America, and a lot of creative people were coming to New York. Olivier Zahm opened an office in New York for *Purple* magazine. France has both an artisanal tradition as well as a culture of doing things with a modern vision. And you understood both sides of it.

CAROL: We tried to bring the essence of France to America in an unexpected way.

ANDRÉ: Yes! You didn't go for the big fashion brands, but went for the really classic brands with history, like St. James and agnés b. All the cool girls used to wear agnés b.'s classic snap cardigan back in the 80s. And you did collaborations with Robert Clergerie and K. Jacques. Clergerie is the classic 80s designer that people forget, but it was also the shit during my time! And K. Jacques, those are the classic St. Tropez sandals. You also had some younger brands like Kitsuné, and you did something with colette, your French equivalent.

HUMBERTO: Every year we do an imaginary Olympics face off. As someone who lives and works in both countries, who do you think wins in USA vs. France?

ANDRÉ: New York has the energy and work ethic to make things happen, and in France we have the naughtiness. New York can be a bit [of a] prude. France works more on feeling and passion than success, money, and career. In that sense I feel close to Opening Ceremony because you have both the passion and a business sense.

HUMBERTO: I think we both work across disciplines. You

do so many things: creative directing for *L'Officiel Hommes*, illustration, making artwork, graffiti; opening nightclubs, hotels, and restaurants.

ANDRÉ: Yes! I think we are now in this period that is similar to La Renaissance. Back then you could be an artist, a scientist, a decorator, a thinker, a writer, and a philosopher. Creation is not one area; it can be everything. You can use every tool. We live in a world where everyone wants to put you in a little box, and I think we are breaking out of that.

CAROL: We've definitely tried to keep the way we work fluid over the years.

ANDRÉ: The way the Opening Ceremony team works is really similar to the way I work. Everything is so organic, so logical. Of course, it's a business, but you don't do things the normal way—you work with friends and family and people who have the same vision. You bring all of this together with the website and the events. It's a platform where everyone can meet. The store has a charming feeling, like an apartment or a house. You can look at books and try some clothes on. It feels like home.

CAROL: And now we are neighbors! Your studio is right nearby, and you will be opening Le Baron in Chinatown.

ANDRÉ: Chinatown still has the feeling of old New York, in the sense that it's still rough and there is a mix of culture. It's not just about the stores—people live and work here, too. Artists live next to a Chinese massage parlor or a gambling place, and you have a gallery next to a fabric store. It's full of creativity.

CAROL: I think we've always thrived off of that creative spirit down here.

HUMBERTO: I'm curious how you see Opening Ceremony as a whole? What do you think has been its impact on the fashion world?

ANDRÉ: It has made fashion more accessible, especially for young kids interested in fashion and culture. When I was a kid, clothing wasn't just a brand, it was an attitude. If you liked punk rock then you dressed like a punk rocker. If you liked New Wave you would dress in black. So it had an impact on not only the way you look, but also the way you live. Clothing represented something that wasn't superficial—it represented who you were.

HUMBERTO: I'm obsessed with the idea of subcultures. Whether it's Karlheinz Weinberger's Swiss rockabilly ▶

kids or Mexican Morrissey fanatics, people that live their looks is always one of my references.

ANDRÉ: Everyone has a look, but what's interesting is what is behind that look and its attitude.

CAROL: One of the other big things we did in 2010 was launch the Opening Ceremony shop at the Ace Hotel. The concept was to create our ideal hotel shop. We travel a lot and have always thought that hotel shops were so lame, and we thought we could do it in an interesting way. So we filled our shop with what we want at a hotel: mini Kiehl's toiletries, the full Criterion DVD Collection, Walkers crisps, Haribo gummies, Band of Outsiders pyjamas....

HUMBERTO: We also launched the corduroy collection with Levi's that year. We've always really cared about bringing back classic American brands.

ANDRÉ: I like that, too. I've always been a big fan of mainstream classic America, and the many little subcultures that it has. Brands like Levi's and Pendleton: when you revisit these classic brands, you bring out the best parts of American fashion. ◆

2010 FRANCE : PARIS

CASA VIGATA
AMAZING PALERMAN FOOD.
44 RUE LÉON FROT, 11th

NANASHI
OUR FRIEND LIONEL'S SPOT THAT SERVES FRESH BENTOS.
57 RUE CHARLOT, 3rd

KRUNG THEP
THEY SAY ITS AS GOOD AS THE FOOD IN THAILAND. ITS AMAZING.
93 RUE JULIEN LACROIX, 20th

THANX GOD I'M A V.I.P.
HEAVEN FOR VINTAGE FANS.
12 RUE DE LANCRY, 10th
thanxgod.com

LE POMPON
GREAT SPOT FOR DANCING !
39 RUE DES PETITES ÉCURIES, 10th
lepomponblog.com

LES BAIN DU MARAIS
PERFECT PLACE FOR A STEAM, SCRUB AND MASSAGE
33, RUE DES BLANCS-MANTEAUX, 4th

My perception of Opening Ceremony is that it has combined commercial success with a visionary risk-taking spirit. It's an organic and authentic approach. Seeing such a personal endeavor succeed is very satisfying, as it shows that faith, hard work, curiosity, and genuine creativity pay off.

EZRA PETRONIO, EDITOR-IN-CHIEF, *SELF SERVICE*; CREATIVE DIRECTOR/FOUNDER, PETRONIO ASSOCIATES

OPENING CEREMONY
Est. 2002

Illustration by André Saraiva for Opening Ceremony, 2011. RIGHT PAGE: France/America sweaters made by Opening Ceremony for Fashion's Night Out, 2010.

OC × agnès b.

One of the most treasured collaborations from the year of France was with agnès b., the influential French designer responsible for turning minimalist basics into the epitome of chic. agnès is perhaps equally renowned as a staunch supporter of some of Opening Ceremony's favorite artists, including Harmony Korine, Dash Snow, and Ryan McGinley. Carol and Humberto visited the forever-young agnès at her lofty white headquarters in Paris and sketched out a line that updates her classic pieces, including striped tees, cotton snap cardigans, and Lolita backpacks.

Opening Ceremony contacted me when they were working on highlighting French designers. They wanted to include some of the agnès b. favorites. I refreshed some of the iconic pieces from my collection: the snap cardigan, the striped t-shirts, and the Fifre jacket. The cool French agnès b. traditionals were reinterpreted by adding new colors and making the silhouettes a bit more fitting. Something we share with Opening Ceremony is the idea of youth, proposing things to this kind of people. I've always loved young people who create themselves and who have talent, whether it's in music, art, or photography.

AGNÈS B., FASHION DESIGNER

OC × Repetto

For the year of France, Opening Ceremony simply had to open the first stateside Repetto shop-in-shop at the New York location, complete with a full range of their favorite ballet flats and tutus, plus a ballet barre and theater seats. But why stop there? Opening Ceremony and Repetto also partnered up to create special co-branded animal printed flats and a Western bootie.

Repetto shoes, Repetto x Opening Ceremony shoes, 2010–2012, photographed for Opening Ceremony. LEFT PAGE, CLOCKWISE FROM TOP LEFT: agnès b. pour Opening Ceremony shopping bag; agnès b. pour Opening Ceremony photographed by Opening Ceremony; OCTV's "Une Pomme Est Une Pomme," 2010.

OC × Deyrolle

While celebrating the year of France, one of Opening Ceremony's most adored destinations in Paris, the historic taxidermy shop Deyrolle, proved an unexpectedly natural choice for collaboration. Carol and Humberto are endlessly inspired by Deyrolle's rooms of flora and fauna curiosities, which provided the basis for printed dresses, scarves, and tops in the women's collection. To create the designs, photographer Bastien Lattanzio photographed Deyrolle's animals, and the prints were then custom altered by Opening Ceremony's designers to create beautifully repeating patterns. With a nod to the idiosyncrasy of the classic spot, the Deyrolle collection captured Opening Ceremony's love for the weird discoveries of travel.

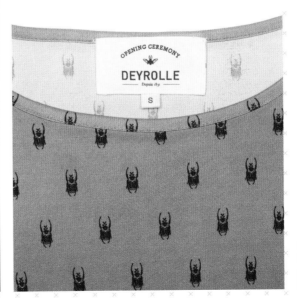

Deyrolle pour Opening Ceremony SS11, photographed by Bastien Lattanzio at Deyrolle.

OC × K. Jacques

Handmade in Saint-Tropez for over eighty years, with a design purity that holds up to its heritage, K. Jacques was a natural choice for an Opening Ceremony collaboration. Taking tried-and-true standbys like the Picon thong sandal and the Homere fisherman sandal, and reworking them in neon, animal print, and iridescent leather for both men and women, K. Jacques pour Opening Ceremony became an instantly updated classic.

OC Introduces Carven

Guillaume Henry took over the reigns at Carven in 2010, infusing this classic Parisian house with a thoroughly fresh and coquettish perspective. Founded in 1945 by Carmen de Tommaso, the brand had been shuttered for several years before Givenchy and Paule Ka alum, Henry took the atelier by storm. High-waisted taffeta shorts, ladylike coats, cropped sweaters, and asymmetrical party dresses fit for gamines quickly became brand signatures.

Carol and Humberto were drawn to his vision from the very first collection, and focused on it for Opening Ceremony's year of France. In 2011, Henry produced a limited-edition dress to commemorate the opening of the Opening Ceremony pop-up shop at Lane Crawford in China. Eager to grow the label, Carven launched its first menswear collection in 2012.

251

Carven SS12, photographed by Jean-Etienne Portail. LEFT PAGE: K. Jacques pour Opening Ceremony 2010–2011, photographed for Opening Ceremony.

OC × Maison Michel

In 2010, Opening Ceremony joined forces with traditional Parisian milliner Maison Michel to create a line of hats and headbands. Chanel's classic hatmaking house, Maison Michel has become newly relevant under the artistic direction of Laetitia Crahay, with pieces such as the bunny and cat ears Mary-Kate and Ashley Olsen wore to Opening Ceremony's Tokyo store opening. The Opening Ceremony collection with Maison Michel included a decadent chainmail headpiece, a quartz-encrusted headband, and a square metal headpiece.

Maison Michel for Opening Ceremony photographed by Karl Lagerfeld, 2011. RIGHT PAGE: Robert Clergerie par Opening Ceremony 2010–2011, photographed for Opening Ceremony.

OC × Robert Clergerie

The continuing Opening Ceremony partnership with revered French shoe designer Robert Clergerie has produced some seriously scintillating footwear. Humberto and his design team traveled to Robert's factory in Romans, France to unearth (and pore over) his archives. The first collection, in spring 2010, was based around the rope-soled platform oxford shoe, which was updated with polka dots, indigo linen, and a custom floral watercolor denim print. Highlights from subsequent collections have included t-strap glittered platform Mary Janes, sky-high velvet heels, and men's shoes with a translucent rubber sole.

OC Introduces Olympia Le-Tan

Olympia Le-Tan's whimsical, literary, hand-embroidered clutches depicting vintage book covers have had a prized place on Opening Ceremony's shelves since day one. Everything she creates is done in a spirit of pure fun, whether it's embroidering a colorful minaudière with a risqué title, making a stop motion movie with Spike Jonze, or singing karaoke with the Opening Ceremony crew in Paris' Belleville neighborhood.

  Olympia started her accessories line in 2009 after stints DJing and singing at Le Baron nightclubs in Paris and Tokyo while designing for Chanel and Gilles Dufour. She was inspired by the old books that her father, illustrator Pierre Le-Tan, piles up in the family's Paris home. Starting with her favorites, she has now stitched her way through a library of wittily-themed collections, recreating the covers of must-reads, medical manuals, and even Shakespeare, all in whimsical felt appliqué. Every bag is hand-cut and sewn in Olympia's atelier, making each one of only a very few numbered and highly sought-after editions.

LEFT: Custom embroidery by Olympia Le-Tan for Opening Ceremony, 2011; Olympia Le-Tan handbags, 2010–2011, photographed by Bruno Werzinski and Opening Ceremony.
RIGHT PAGE: Artwork by Aurel Schmidt, courtesy of the artist, 2010; T-shirts by Aurel Schmidt for Opening Ceremony.

OC × Aurel Schmidt

Opening Ceremony paired with downtown New York artist Aurel Schmidt for a line of t-shirts that spelled out O-P-E-N-I-N-G C-E-R-E-M-O-N-Y using her signature illustrative style of detailed drawings of bits of debris like cigarette butts and banana peels. To congratulate Aurel on being included in the 2010 Whitney Biennial, we dipped the tees in resin and hung them in the window of the New York store.

We opened our dream hotel gift shop at the Ace Hotel in New York!

As the consummate world travelers, Carol and Humberto were only too happy to create their ideal hotel shop at the Ace Hotel in Manhattan. Opening Ceremony's second New York location, the Ace Hotel shop is a creatively tiny space dedicated to ideal souvenirs and fashion, including Haribo snacks, Walkers Crisps, McSweeney's books, Kiehl's travel sets, The Criterion Collection DVDs, and exclusive Tumi luggage. In February 2010, the petite shop opened with a massive party at the hotel, highlighted by a now-legendary performance by Solange Knowles and the Dirty Projectors.

Opening Ceremony feels like a funhouse where, around each corner, there's something super cool to explore. It's the only store where I will bring my eight-year-old son to shop with me, because I know he will get a kick out of a lot of things there. There's always a really strong sense of adolescent energy.

SOLANGE KNOWLES, MUSICIAN

LEFT: Solange Knowles and Dirty Projectors performing at the Ace Hotel opening party; RIGHT AND RIGHT PAGE: Opening Ceremony at Ace Hotel photographed by Michael Vahrenwald, 2012.

Choosing who would occupy the Ace Hotel space was like having an apartment and figuring out who would be good roommates.

ALEX CALDERWOOD, CO-FOUNDER, ACE HOTEL

OC × Rob Pruitt

Artist Rob Pruitt swung far into the Opening Ceremony orbit in 2010. First, inspired by a conversation with Humberto, Rob created a collection of his ultimate dream t-shirts, which he also immortalized as silkscreened paintings for a coinciding exhibition at the gallery Gavin Brown's Enterprise. Next, Rob created a flea market installation at Opening Ceremony at the Ace Hotel. All the proceeds from the flea market sales went to support the The Trevor Project for LGBT youth.

Rob Pruitt's Flea Market

Join Rob Pruitt and Opening Ceremony for an afternoon flea market and reception

Opening Ceremony at Ace Hotel
1190–1192 Broadway
Saturday, October 9th, from 1–4pm

Rob Pruitt
glitter
$25/bag
$100—
signed

TOP: Flyer for Rob Pruitt's Flea Market; CENTER: Still from Spike Jonze's video of Rob and Humberto at Flea Market; BOTTOM: Glitter for sale. RIGHT PAGE: Rob Pruitt x Opening Ceremony t-shirts. PREVIOUS SPREAD: Opening Ceremony at Ace Hotel photographed by Michael Vahrenwald, 2012.

Rob Pruitt photographed
by Terry Richardson,
2011. RIGHT PAGE: Rob
Pruitt's bag of glitter,
photographed by Zoë
Ghertner, 2011.

OC × Levi's

Beginning in 2010, Opening Ceremony has paired with the classic San Francisco-based denim company, Levi's, on three exclusive collections. Pairing the tried-and-true workmanship of Levi's with Opening Ceremony's design innovations, the collections share an unexpected update on standards such as jean jackets and chambray shirts. For the inaugural season, in Spring 2010, Opening Ceremony transformed Levi's cords, with corduroy basics redone in golden mustard, turquoise, and fuchsia. To launch this first season, the Opening Ceremony team went to San Francisco for a bash, and promoted the line by wrapping bikes and outdoor signs in corduroy. Fall 2010 delved into denim, with a Sherpa-lined denim bomber and striped 505s. In Spring 2011, Terry Richardson shot the collection, which focused heavily on chambray in a range of sherbet shades.

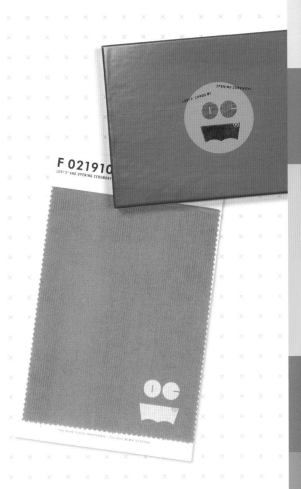

CLOCKWISE FROM TOP LEFT: Wooden display dolls wearing miniature Levi's for Opening Ceremony; Team member Gillian Tozer wearing the collection; Campaign ephemera; Pop-up store window, San Francisco. LEFT PAGE AND FOLLOWING SPREAD: Levi's for Opening Ceremony SS10.

Levi's for Opening
Ceremony, SS11,
photographed by Terry
Richardson. RIGHT PAGE:
Levi's for Opening
Ceremony FW10,
photographed by
Opening Ceremony.

OC × Hickey Freeman

Hickey Freeman, the traditional American suitmaker, paired with Opening Ceremony in 2010 for an exclusive line of suiting, reimagined for a new generation of sartorially-savvy men. Combining tried-and-true Hickey Freeman craftsmanship and tradition with a scaled-down fit, the partnership goes beyond retro to be forward-looking. To launch the collection, Hickey Freeman and Opening Ceremony asked photographer Bill Gentle of the *Backyard Bill* website to shoot the looks on creative men, such as artist Marc Hundley and photographer Michael Hauptman, in their homes. The continuing partnership now includes tuxedos for a slightly hipper red carpet moment.

Marc Hundley in Hickey
Freeman & Opening
Ceremony FW10. LEFT PAGE,
CLOCKWISE FROM TOP LEFT:
Hickey Freeman & Opening
Ceremony embroidery;
Ferdinando Verderi; Kyle
Thurman; Andrew Long;
Michael Hauptman; Sinisa
Mackovic, all wearing
Hickey Freeman & Opening
Ceremony FW10, all
photographed by Bill Gentle.

271

OC × Jean Paul Gaultier

When Opening Ceremony featured France, we dipped deep into Jean Paul Gaultier's reservoir of innovative designs. A trendsetter among French designers for over 25 years, Gaultier was not only responsible for Madonna's bustier, but also for bringing the avant-garde Parisian underground to global recognition. Opening Ceremony began by buying extensively from his ready-to-wear collections before producing an exclusively co-branded line of stripy Matelot t-shirts with JEAN PAUL GAULTIER POUR OPENING CEREMONY etched into the stripes. Humberto even convinced the Gaultier team to reissue a super-limited-edition of the chunky Pataugas sneakers that he had once spied in a storefront in Paris.

JEANPAULGAULTIER POUR OPENING CEREMONY

'10 FR

OC × *Tron: Legacy*

Looking beyond the world of fashion, Opening Ceremony partnered with Disney for the TRON: Legacy Opening Ceremony collection in fall 2010. Inspired by the film *TRON: Legacy*, a sequel to the 1982 cult flick *TRON*, the collection featured high-tech aesthetics utilizing neon, neoprene, and laser cuts. Also awesome was the three-way collaboration with ThreeAsFour featuring a revival of the brand's retro-futuristic circle bag.

TOP: *TRON: Legacy* Opening Ceremony hangtag; CENTER: New York store window; BOTTOM: *TRON: Legacy* Opening Ceremony photographed by Opening Ceremony. LEFT PAGE, TOP: Jean Paul Gaultier pour Opening Ceremony, Pataugas sneaker; BOTTOM: Jean Paul Gaultier FW10 shirt, photographed by Opening Ceremony. FOLLOWING TWO SPREADS: Opening Ceremony SS10, photographed by David Benjamin Sherry.

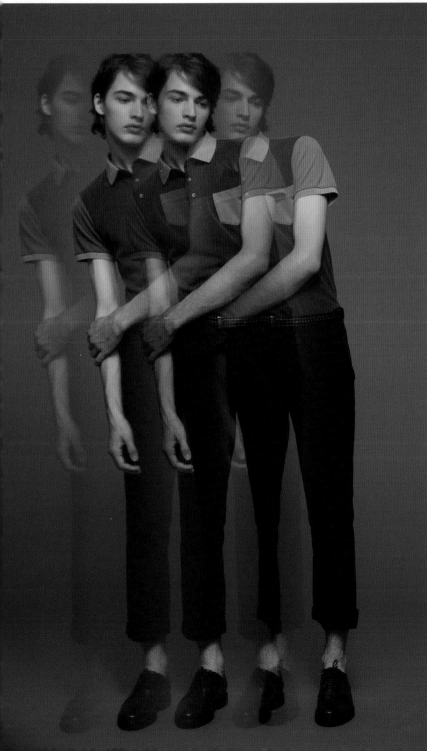

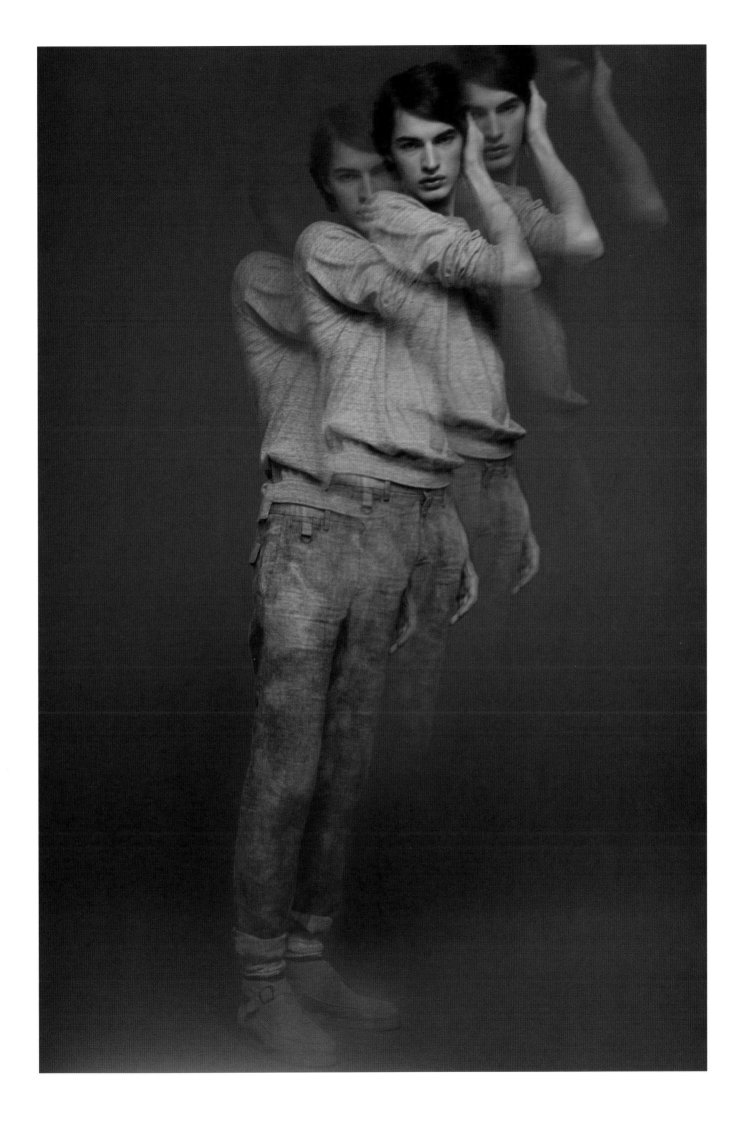

OPENING CEREMONY

Est. 2002

openingceremony.us

We launched *OCTV*, our own online television channel!

OCTV, the online television channel and video production arm of Opening Ceremony, was founded in 2010 to create and support quirky, DIY films. In-house directors and producers, as well as a cast of guest directors including Spike Jonze, Gia Coppola, Aaron Rose, Carlos Charlie Perez, and Lisa Rovner, have created original work revolving around the Opening Ceremony experience, collectively reimagining what a fashion film can be. *OCTV* has featured cooking videos with David Chang of Momofuku and Wylie Dufresne of wd~50, a peek inside Chloë Sevigny's closets, and a film for Target's GO International Designer Collective starring a high school step team from the Bronx, in addition to playfully nontraditional fashion videos and commercials shot around the world. With over six million viewers and nominations in several film festivals within the first year after its founding, *OCTV* is one of the most exciting developing areas of the company.

OCTV videos, **CLOCKWISE FROM TOP:** "Step! Clap! Go!," 2011; "Perfect Scrambled Eggs with Wylie Dufresne," 2011; "OC Intimates Commercials," 2011. **RIGHT PAGE:** *OCTV*'s "The World is Yours," 2011. **PREVIOUS TWO SPREADS:** Opening Ceremony FW10, photographed by Max Farago.

The World Is Yours

AARON ROSE, CURATOR/FILMMAKER

When I used to live in New York, I always took Crosby Street when walking downtown. This quiet little street, which runs north-south and parallel between Broadway and Lafayette Streets, was a haven where I could gather my thoughts. It was a welcome alternative to the hustle and bustle of the busy shopping streets on either side of it. I've always loved this street because it was pretty much assured that I wouldn't run into anyone I knew. It was *my* street—and as anyone that has ever spent time in New York knows, alone time is a precious commodity. So, imagine my surprise when one day on my walk I saw a notice that a new clothing store was coming in. My first thought, of course, was, "There goes the neighborhood." However, that sentiment would soon change.

I can't remember the first time I walked into Opening Ceremony, but the feeling I had that day is still with me. The place was most definitely a clothing store, but it felt more like a workshop, or maybe a think tank. There was a creative energy in the place that seemed to both inspire and educate. The work of clothing designers, books, and small art objects on display were the cutting edge of what was being created at that time. Now, ten years later, this hasn't changed a bit. Opening Ceremony has always been about fashion at its best. Every time I've ever stepped foot in one of their shops, I've walked out with a whole new list of amazing creations the world has to offer. I think a big part of that comes from the overwhelming spirit of collaboration at the heart of the Opening Ceremony project.

In 2011, I had the honor of taking part in one of these fantastic collaborations. Rory Satran and Humberto Leon approached me to contribute some video content to their recently launched online TV channel, *OCTV*. I had been invited to go to Guayaquil, Ecuador for a film festival, and so I proposed the idea of collaborating with *OCTV* on a film down there. Now, this was a real stretch of a production as none of us knew anyone in Ecuador—all we had seen were online images of this beautiful neighborhood called Las Peñas, which was a neon-painted favela on a hill over the city. After a few discussions, we decided to make it happen, not knowing how we were going to do it, just trusting that the potential was great. The film was to be a love story titled *El Mundo Es Tuyo (The World Is Yours)*. For a month before production, we combed the Internet, using Facebook and Twitter to find Opening Ceremony fans in Ecuador who could help us with our shoot. After a week or so, we had found our actors and pulled together a haphazard but extremely enthusiastic crew. Even though we had not yet met anyone, in person, who was going to work on this, we all knew that something great was going to happen.

A few weeks later we landed in Ecuador. I brought a camera and a bunch of gear and Rory showed up from New York with a giant suitcase of clothes. We met our Ecuador team the next morning for coffee and immediately sprung into action. The shoot was the next day and we had our work cut out for us. Our new pals immediately got on the phone and started calling in more friends of theirs to help. We divided and conquered, and ended up putting together the most amazing DIY production I've ever worked on. Our production designer, Cristina, even built a crazy rain machine using nothing but 2x4s and a garden hose! You cannot imagine the scene we had going on. We had streets closed in this crazy little village, with cars honking and people screaming at us in Spanish. In order to get water for the rain machine, we had to pay off the local street cleaners to come with their pressure washer. The whole thing was totally nuts! However, I can honestly say that working on that film was one of the most fun times I've had making art in my life. That is a real testament to the philosophy and working methods of Opening Ceremony.

When I think back to those early days on Crosby Street, and the fact that I was initially saddened by the arrival of a fashion store on my private walk, I now have to chuckle. Today, I cannot imagine Crosby and Howard without Opening Ceremony. They were the perfect addition to that street and came at a time when New York City really needed it. Now, the fact that they have managed to spread that amazing creative spirit across the world is truly a gift. ◆

Our old office above the Howard Street store got slightly crowded...

Office interiors
photographed by
Michael Vahrenwald,
2012. TOP RIGHT:
Carol and Humberto
photographed by Jason
Frank Rothenberg.
PREVIOUS SPREAD: Office
at 35 Howard Street.

...so we moved into sweet new digs
on Centre Street.

We have been proud to support the incredible film projects of friends and heroes.

Carol and Humberto's passion for film has informed Opening Ceremony's support of movie projects. Beyond large-scale collaborations like *Where the Wild Things Are* and *TRON: Legacy*, Opening Ceremony has made its stores cultural centers with a myriad of screenings, signings, and limited-edition products. For the 2008 release of Wong Kar-wai's film *My Blueberry Nights*, Opening Ceremony paired with the film's legendary director to produce a collection of postcards, t-shirts, and posters featuring his personal snapshots of deep America taken during the filming. In 2010, Opening Ceremony bestie Spike Jonze did a store window and screening with the store for his short robot love story, *I'm Here*. He and a bear-costumed Marcel Dzama also did an experiential talk/musical performance for *There Are Many of Us*, the film's accompanying book. For the premiere of Mike Mills' 2011 film *Beginners*, Opening Ceremony celebrated by creating an exclusive line of sweatshirts, hosting an in-store book signing for a collection of drawings from the movie, and presenting the film's New York premiere. And artist and filmmaker Miranda July promoted her 2011 movie *The Future* on the Opening Ceremony blog, releasing a special interview with a psychic and also by creating a special "Forgetting Napkin"—intended to mend a broken heart—as a contest giveaway.

I'm not a frequent clothing shopper and everyone who works at Opening Ceremony is so personable, friendly, and informative—the opposite of what you would expect from a store with such hipster credentials; no indie record store snobbery. There were many brands I had never heard of that fit my smaller frame, which had been challenging. It was a major revelation to discover brands that would fit off of the rack.

ELIJAH WOOD, ACTOR

LEFT: *I'm Here* by Spike Jonze, 2010; RIGHT: OCTV's "Non Plus One" by Gia Coppola, 2010. RIGHT PAGE, CLOCKWISE FROM TOP LEFT: Mike Mills at the New York store, 2011; Mike Mills x Opening Ceremony sweatshirt; Miranda July and Humberto; Miranda July's "Forgetting Napkin"; *Somewhere* limited-edition poster designed by Peter Miles, signed by director Sofia Coppola; *I'm Here* flipbooks; Spike Jonze and the OC team; Wong Kar-wai for Opening Ceremony t-shirt. CENTER: Wong Kar-wai with Carol and Humberto.

This napkin is covering a picture of a person I am trying to forget.

25 POSTCARDS

MY BLUEBERRY NIGHTS
PHOTOGRAPHS BY WONG KAR WAI

NEW YORK

My Blueberry Nights
postcard book with
photographs by Wong
Kar-wai, photographed
by Zoë Ghertner, 2011.
RIGHT PAGE: Jason
Schwartzman photographed
by Terry Richardson, 2011;
INSET: *OCTV*'s "Jason
Schwartzman for OC Tokyo"
by Matt Wolf, 2009.

You don't really need to buy anything at Opening Ceremony and it's still a fun experience. Just looking at things and talking to all the people who work there...It's really nice. Clothes, music, or anything at its best is just a collection of ideas. That's why I like going to the store: it's a collection of people's ideas. Carol and Humberto seem happy because they get to try new things. I don't think they subscribe to the idea that everything has to be miserable, stressful, or a terrible experience for work to get done. They try to get stuff done in a happier way. They love new things and they're constantly interested, and therefore, they're interesting, which comes across with Opening Ceremony.

JASON SCHWARTZMAN, ACTOR

2011

ARGENTINA

Jen Brill photographed by
Terry Richardson, 2011.

Jen Brill with Carol and Humberto on 2011

Carol and Humberto sit down with their Chinatown neighbor, Jen Brill, in a café on Baxter Street to talk about the incomparable creative nexus of their shared corner in New York City. A true multi-hyphenate, Jen is a creative consultant, Chanel ambassador, and board member for RxArt, a non-profit bringing contemporary art into hospitals. With her gift for connecting talent, Jen has orbited around the Opening Ceremony universe since its earliest days.

JEN: 2011 was such a big year for you guys, with collaborations with Rodarte and Maison Martin Margiela and your appointment as creative directors of Kenzo. As someone who has known you guys and been around the store for so long, it was really satisfying to see your work and talents recognized on the world stage.

HUMBERTO: This year, there was definitely a sense of coming into a new era.

JEN: We're all relatively the same age and we've been in the same downtown world for a while. I lived on Grand and Centre Street, right near the store, in 2003. Back then, there was literally nothing on Howard Street aside for Opening Ceremony.

CAROL: You're a lifelong New Yorker. As suburban kids, Humberto and I have always had a real fascination with the idea of growing up in the city. What were some of the stores that you would come downtown to visit, and how do you think Opening Ceremony compares to them?

JEN: I started exploring downtown because it represented freedom: you could dress however you wanted, do whatever you wanted. I'd look at the back pages of *The Village Voice* and *Paper* magazine, which were the bibles for what was going on downtown and what was cool. As an Upper East Side 8th grader, the stores I was most excited to go downtown to visit were X-Girl, Supreme, Liquid Sky, Final Home, Unique, Mary Frey's ice cream shop, Guru Sno-Balls. I would walk into Liquid Sky wearing my school uniform to buy a long sleeved t-shirt with an alien on it, feeling like such an Upper East Side nerd. Patricia Fields' House of Field on 8th Street was an incredible place. The first thing you saw walking into that shop was the makeup counter, with the trannies and crossdressers getting ready to go out. Those stores were cultural experiences. And I think that Opening Ceremony is a lot like that, too.

HUMBERTO: We've always thought that there was some kind of lineage that connected us to those 90s stores downtown. We think of our stores as cultural spaces, where kids can come in from the suburbs and learn a little more about what's going on in the city.

JEN: A lot of those stores sold music and gave out club flyers, and I feel like people stopped doing that. At Opening Ceremony, you still sell books and music.

CAROL: The idea is that a kid will come in and be able to take away a little piece of Opening Ceremony, even if they can't afford the Christopher Kane dress. There's just something for everyone.

JEN: I can see how the store is inspired by you two growing up with mall culture. It's very Asian, as well, with its souvenir shopping concept. Your shopping experience in Hong Kong was a huge inspiration in opening the store, right?

HUMBERTO: Yes! Carol and I traveled to Hong Kong and wanted to bring back to New York the effusive, passionate approach to shopping that we found there. That's how the store was born.

CAROL: Which is why it was so exciting to open our pop-up stores at Lane Crawford in Hong Kong and Shanghai in 2011. It was like coming full circle.

JEN: My mom lives in Hong Kong, and you guys invited her to the opening of the pop-ups. It was a really proud moment for me, because it was on a level that she could really understand what my friends were doing.

CAROL: It's nice to be able to share these big events with our families.

JEN: It makes me think of the way you collaborate with artists. With friends like Aurel Schmidt, Ryan McGinley, Terence Koh...everyone is hanging out, so there's a dialogue, right? There's nothing better than working with people that you love and that interest you.

CAROL: Totally. When we look at our friends across all different disciplines, whether it's Ryan or Terence in art, Jack and Lazaro of Proenza Schouler or Kate and Laura of Rodarte in fashion, or Karen O in music, we sense that they are part of the same generation.

JEN: We have the same references. There's a reason why we all know each other and we orbit around this Opening Ceremony bulb. It's because there's so much common ground.

HUMBERTO: When we remade the classic cotton Lolita ▶

backpack with agnès b., I had to tell you right away because I knew you would get it!

JEN: There's a certain amount of nostalgia in Opening Ceremony. You take the things we were obsessed with as kids and breathe new life into them for a new generation.

CAROL: That's important for us. And since we're always pulling out these things from our youth, whether it's a Lolita bag or original Dr. Martens, it's important that we explain their relevance, which we try and do through the blog.

JEN: The blog is amazing! If I were an 18-year-old in Louisiana and all I had was my computer, I'd be so obsessed with that blog.

HUMBERTO: It's like a large-scale version of Liquid Sky giving out rave flyers. We're trying to create a megaphone for our interests. 2011 was the year we featured Argentina, and the blog was a great way of sharing our finds and travel stories from the country.

CAROL: When we traveled there we concentrated on local, artisanal products and the amazing food. Argentina was a return to the way we featured countries at the beginning of Opening Ceremony, by bringing back souvenirs. We brought back suitcases filled with everything we loved from the *mercado*: leather flasks, handmade rugs, pompom earrings....

JEN: It had that personal touch, as though your friend went to Argentina and brought back the coolest stuff!

CAROL: We're always trying to balance the roots of Opening Ceremony by expanding to a larger audience. Another thing that was really exciting in 2011 was working on our lookbooks with two photographers that you've worked closely with: Terry Richardson and Theo Wenner.

JEN: Terry was probably one of the few fashion photographers that any of us knew about as teenagers. His studio is such a crossroads in New York City, with all the different characters, the energy, the way he stops people on the street and takes a picture.... He's about making images that inspire him, and there are no rules in the way he works. And that feels similar to the way Opening Ceremony works: instinctively. You're constantly opening doors and forging relationships with talented people. People always ask me what the secret is to your success; I think it's family, love, compassion, genuine interest, enthusiasm, and this fire that is just so real. Whether it's finding a new Chinese restaurant in Flushing or producing an incredible fashion show, there is a true curiosity. ◆

Opening Ceremony knows about what's it, and Argentina is definitely it! They showed us we can make some noise in the international fashion scene, despite our far-flung location.

SOFIA SANCHEZ BARRENECHEA,
ART DIRECTOR, ENTREPRENEUR

In Argentina, we visited dozens of hidden markets to find local artisanal gems for our stores!

The Opening Ceremony team traveled to Argentina several times in 2011. These trips were ruled by visits to *el mercado*, to scour the local artisan stands for rare, handmade, exclusive finds to bring back to New York. The market experience was replicated with an online *El Mercadito* shop showcasing the best finds, arranged in a *muy auténtico* tableau.

TOP: Opening Ceremony team in Buenos Aires; MIDDLE, BOTTOM: El Mercado on the Opening Ceremony website. FOLLOWING TWO SPREADS: Opening Ceremony SS11, photographed by Terry Richardson. PAGES 302–305: Opening Ceremony FW11, photographed by Theo Wenner.

OPENING
CEREMONY

OPENINGCEREMONY.US

301

OC × Lane Crawford

Returning to the land of Humberto and Carol's first trip together, and the birthplace of the idea for the company, Opening Ceremony partnered with Hong Kong retail giant Lane Crawford in the spring of 2011. For four weeks, Lane Crawford department stores in Hong Kong and Beijing hosted Opening Ceremony pop-up shops, with exclusive pieces from Alexander Wang, Carven, Band of Outsiders, Suno, and Pamela Love. Carol, Humberto, their moms, Chloë Sevigny, and much of the Opening Ceremony team traveled to Hong Kong, Beijing, and Shanghai for a whirlwind tour that included launch parties for the pop-ups, a walk down the Great Wall of China, and of course, a whole lot of eating!

Lane Crawford store interiors courtesy of Lane Crawford. LEFT PAGE, TOP: Opening Ceremony team at Lane Crawford Hong Kong. PREVIOUS SPREAD: Opening Ceremony men's FW11, photographed by Gia Coppola.

309

OC × Rodarte

Rodarte for Opening Ceremony is a special collaboration between Humberto, Carol, and Rodarte founders Kate and Laura Mulleavy. The former Berkeley classmates teamed up to produce two full men's, women's, and accessories collections in spring and fall 2011, documented with indelible imagery by frequent Rodarte collaborator Autumn de Wilde.

**Rodarte for Opening
Ceremony SS11,
photographed by
Autumn de Wilde.**
FOLLOWING SPREAD:
**Rodarte for Opening
Ceremony FW11,
photographed by
Autumn de Wilde.**

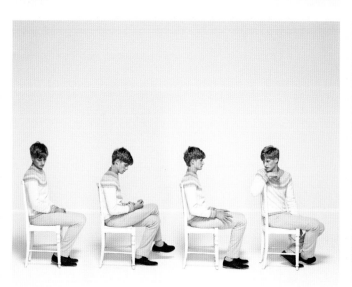

OC Introduces J.W. Anderson...

J.W. Anderson has been buzz-worthy since his 2007 London debut, where his models wore jewelry incorporating real insects. Even in those early menswear collections, Anderson's special talent lay in toeing the line between sinister and sweet, tough and feminine. Soon, women were borrowing pieces from their boyfriends and, due to popular demand, in 2009 Anderson began showing womenswear. As in his men's collections, the designer has developed a look that lies somewhere in between grunge and schoolgirl. Whether it's sparkly grinder boots or pants with skirts, every season Anderson presents something a little rebellious.

Joseph Altuzarra...

Joseph Altuzarra left his native Paris for the States to study art and art history at Swarthmore College. Soon after, he scored an internship with Marc Jacobs, and leaping from success to success, Altuzarra then freelanced for Proenza Schouler, before returning to Paris for a spell at Givenchy. If that sounds impressive, it is. Even more so because when the designer started his own line in 2009, he was only 25-years-old.

Not only have Carol and Humberto stocked the designer's coveted parkas and power dresses from the beginning of his brand, but his Walker Street studio also used to be Humberto's apartment. Joseph's mother, Karen, has even modeled for the Opening Ceremony website, and when Joseph's prodigious talents were recognized by a CFDA Fashion Award in 2011, everyone at OC looked on like proud family.

When I started my own label, I knew I wanted to sell at Opening Ceremony. Carol and Humberto made an appointment to see the collection, and when they got to our office Humberto realized our space had once been his apartment. It was fate!

JOSEPH ALTUZARRA

TOP: J.W. Anderson SS11, photographed by Opening Ceremony; BOTTOM: Altuzarra FW11, photographed by Opening Ceremony. RIGHT PAGE: Mary Katrantzou FW11, photographed by Opening Ceremony.

...and Mary Katrantzou

Whether she's referencing Fabergé eggs, Babe Paley, or Imperial China, Mary Katrantzou manages to captivate her audience with her digitized trompe l'oeil patterns and out-of-this-world colors. Born in Greece, Mary grew up surrounded by textiles. Inspired by the fabrics and shapes that emerged from her mother's furniture factory, Mary studied architecture at RISD and interior design at Central Saint Martins. She soon switched to fashion prints and graduated from Central Saint Martins in 2008, starting her eponymous line that same year to great fanfare. The London designer's extravagantly printed pieces quickly captured the Opening Ceremony team's imaginations, and we snapped her up in 2011.

OC × MM6 Maison Martin Margiela

MM6 Maison Martin Margiela x Opening Ceremony is the elusive Paris-based fashion house's first-ever partnership with another design company. For Fall 2011, Opening Ceremony paired with the conceptually adventurous MM6 to produce a full line of women's clothing and accessories that adopts a three-in-one approach, with interchangeable mix-and-match elements within each garment, including boots that come with sewn-in leather stirrups, white dress shirts buttoned into black blazers, and sleeveless dresses layered over long-sleeved dresses. These core concepts of transformation broaden the 20 original styles into a potential multitude of different silhouettes.

"Pixel Geometry with Hannelore Knuts" animated gif online editorial by Goodsy (Jason Oliver Goodman). LEFT PAGE: Opening Ceremony x MM6 Maison Martin Margiela FW11, photographed by Opening Ceremony.

OC × Reyn Spooner

Opening Ceremony revamped the traditional Hawaiian shirt with its Reyn Spooner collaboration. Introducing a more subtle take on Hawaiian style, Reyn McCullough has looked to traditional woodblock and reverse print methods to create his signature sophisticated Aloha shirting since 1962. As long-time fans, Opening Ceremony had the great pleasure of sifting through the Reyn Spooner archives to select vintage fabrics for this collaborative collection for men and women. Actress Kirsten Dunst went on tour with the band Jenny and Johnny and sent back some snapshots of the whole gang in Reyn Spooner outfits.

TOP: *OCTV*'s "22" by Gia Coppola, 2011; **BOTTOM:** Reyn Spooner for Opening Ceremony SS11, photographed by Opening Ceremony. **RIGHT PAGE:** Kirsten Dunst wearing Reyn Spooner for Opening Ceremony SS11, photographed by Jason Boesel.

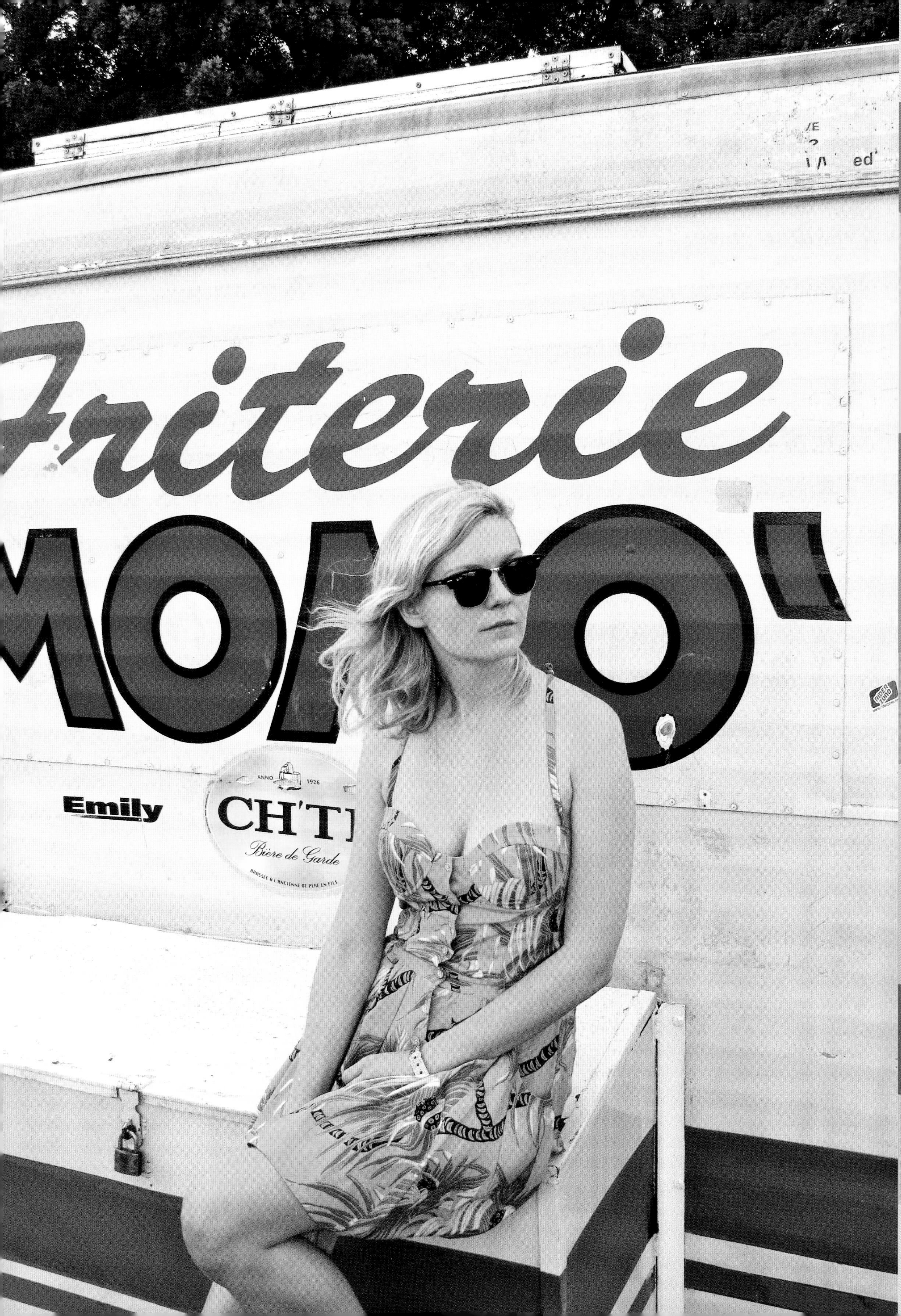
Friterie
Emily
ANNO 1926
Bière de Garde

Supporting equality and causes we believe in has been an important part of Opening Ceremony.

Opening Ceremony's commitment to causes is deeply organic and reactive, and gay equality causes are particularly dear to the company. Opening Ceremony's t-shirt partnership with legendary AIDS activism group ACT UP features reissues of classic ACT UP and Gran Fury designs from the 80s, with proceeds supporting the organizations. When New York adopted same-sex marriage equality in 2011, Opening Ceremony created a celebratory t-shirt, modeled on Opening Ceremony staffers and their partners.

Working with queer musicians, artists, and designers has been an important and visible part of Opening Ceremony's business. This is of huge importance to the queer community not only in New York, but all over the world. Over the years it has been both uplifting and inspiring to watch Opening Ceremony collaborate with Act Up to create a reissued t-shirt line, include Pride events into their schedule, and consistently cover queer content and news on their blog.

JD SAMSON, MUSICIAN, ARTIST

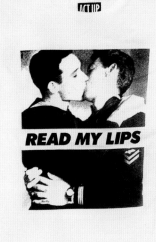

CLOCKWISE FROM TOP LEFT: Opening Ceremony "Love is Equal" t-shirts on Ed Brachfeld and Benjamin Gaspard, photographed for Opening Ceremony; Opening Ceremony ACT UP t-shirts photographed for Opening Ceremony.

OC × Japan

When Japan was struck by an earthquake and tsunami in 2011, Opening Ceremony created a limited-edition t-shirt to support Red Cross relief efforts in the country. The t-shirts were modeled by Rinko Kikuchi and Jenny Shimizu in an impromptu photo shoot by Tim Barber on our office's rooftop, and debuted at a gala benefit party at The Standard Hotel.

I participated as one of the hosts for the Japan tsunami charity event that Opening Ceremony organized. I thought the cause was very noble and the t-shirt was great, too. Of course, being Japanese, I was happy to be able to contribute.

RINKO KIKUCHI, ACTOR

OC × The Muppets

Coinciding with the release of *The Muppets* movie, The Muppets x Opening Ceremony collection featured the lovable felt gang wearing Opening Ceremony men's and women's button-downs, sweaters, hoodies, and t-shirts. The collection was playfully presented at Fashion's Night Out in September 2011, with Miss Piggy interviewing Carol and Humberto. The ever diva-ish star demanded the spotlight, of course, so the Opening Ceremony store in Los Angeles put up a billboard featuring a reclining Miss Piggy. To complete the collaboration, a beautiful, mechanical Muppets château graced our New York store window.

© THE MUPPETS STUDIO, LLC

TOP: Autographed photo of Miss Piggy; MIDDLE: Miss Piggy billboard at Opening Ceremony Los Angeles; BOTTOM: The Muppets wearing Opening Ceremony, illustration by Disney Muppets and Opening Ceremony. RIGHT PAGE: The Muppets x Opening Ceremony FW11, photographed by Opening Ceremony.

©Disney

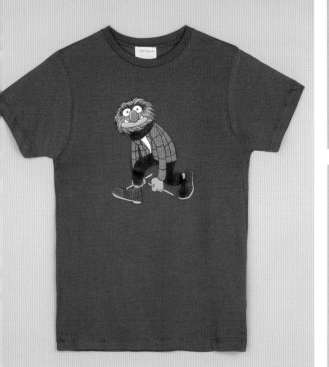

OC × A for Apple

The apple never falls far from the tree! Case in point: Opening Ceremony by A for Apple, a kidswear collection created in partnership with the Hong Kong-based children's apparel brand. The playful collection offers classic Opening Ceremony designs, including the gaudet dress, flare coat, and patchwork shirt, remade in the tiniest of cuts.

Opening Ceremony
+
a for apple

Opening Ceremony and A for Apple collection, photographed by Ingalls Photography.

La Manzana

La Carne

2012

KOREA

Kate and Laura Mulleavy
photographed by Terry
Richardson, 2011.

Kate and Laura Mulleavy with Carol and Humberto on 2012

Humberto and Carol share many parallels with Kate and Laura Mulleavy of the innovative fashion brand Rodarte. Starting as students at University of California at Berkeley during an overlapping period, and later as fellow fashion pioneers, the four Californians have remained close friends throughout the years. Kate and Laura founded Rodarte in 2005, and the label was soon picked up by their former classmates at Opening Ceremony, before Rodarte went on to become a leading force in fashion and art. A limited-edition collaborative collection, Rodarte for Opening Ceremony, was launched for 2011. Kate, Laura, Humberto, and Carol discuss the past ten years, and what the future may hold in 2012 and beyond.

KATE: We all knew each other at UC Berkeley. We were a creative group of people and there was a camaraderie between us....

CAROL: Totally. Berkeley is the least fashion-oriented place you can imagine, but it produced all these people who ended up working in fashion.

LAURA: Fashion is a form of storytelling. Being at a school that had so little to do with fashion in the traditional sense was most fitting for the way we think of things. Berkeley is a place where you interact with people much more than in a city like Los Angeles or even New York. You get to know all the characters—and there are a lot of characters out there! I think that interaction sparked our imaginations more than traditional ideas of fashion and beauty. At Berkeley, you're exposed to so many different things and you really get to see how complex the world of aesthetics is.

HUMBERTO: Right, and it definitely fostered curiosity. Mixing things like art, literature, and science seemed like an important thing. What were you doing between graduating from Berkeley and starting Rodarte in 2005?

KATE: Laura and I finished school and moved back to Los Angeles, where our parents were living. At that point we realized that we wanted to go into fashion. It wasn't something that was a new revelation, we just didn't go to school for it. We took a year or two to study things on our own and think about what we wanted to do. It was such a weird time period because we were really obsessed with horror films, and watched so many of them. It's really indicative of the way we do things. We thrive on wanting to know more about something on a more complicated level.

HUMBERTO: I totally relate to that tendency to geek-out over stuff. Has your design process remained the same since the beginning?

KATE: From the first collection to now, our design process has always been instinctual. Laura and I are very broad in our inspirations, but also very insular in how we create. We really don't want to know what other people are doing and we don't look at other designers. When I look at a dress, I'll know that I designed that from some place in my imagination.

CAROL: I think that's one of the parallels between Rodarte and Opening Ceremony: creating instinctually. Everything we do is ruled by emotion and doesn't follow a typical business model.

LAURA: I can see that. And by working instinctually you have opened so many doors, in terms of what retailing can mean. It's heartfelt, and I don't think there's a formula for that.

HUMBERTO: Opening Ceremony's formula is to not follow a formula! Since we have known each other for so long and always connected creatively, it was only a matter of time before we started collaborating beyond selling Rodarte in the store. So we came together to create a limited-edition Rodarte for Opening Ceremony line.

LAURA: We designed two seasons—spring and fall 2011. It was like a college reunion for us. We got to work with different people and experience the world of Opening Ceremony in a different way. I look at the two seasons and I think that we made a very special capsule with you, and that was really, really fun!

CAROL: It really was. We're all from California, and Opening Ceremony is a real blend of east and west coasts. Rodarte often references California's nature and history. What specifically about your work is Californian? How can this essence be distilled?

KATE: California has had such an impact on our design aesthetic, and I think that our thought process is connected to the landscape.

LAURA: In Los Angeles, there is this strange freedom that you can always leave to go to other places, like Joshua Tree, which is an alien landscape, or the Redwood forests, which have the largest trees in the world.

CAROL: California can feel like a bunch of different countries.

HUMBERTO: The Olympics have always been a huge part of Opening Ceremony, and in 2012 they will be in London. ▸

I remember that amazing portfolio you guys did with Ryan McGinley, where you made custom garments for Olympians.

KATE: It was great working with Ryan. Laura would call and talk to the athletes and find out what was possible to wear. Sports are based on aerodynamics, so if you add a little bit of weight to the garment, it affects the performance. It was amazing to work with such incredible people.

CAROL: Did working with athletes on the Olympics project help you to prepare for making the ballet costumes for the movie *Black Swan*?

LAURA: We were actually doing those at the same time. Looking back, I don't know how we physically did it. The projects were so different because with *Black Swan* we were working, alongside actors and a director and everyone else that was involved in the film, to create characters. And with the Olympics, we were just trying to find a way to visually enhance something these athletes were already doing.

HUMBERTO: Both Opening Ceremony and Rodarte are based on really fruitful professional partnerships. I wouldn't be able to work without Carol, and vice versa. How do the two of you work together?

KATE: Laura and I are pieces of a larger whole, and we design as one person. The only thing different that I do apart from Laura is make the final sketches. People always ask who does what, and I don't think it's that simple. It's not a mathematical equation.

CAROL: It is the same with my partnership with Humberto: you can't separate us. We both have a vision of Opening Ceremony and where we want it to go, and that almost lives on its own at this point. So let's go back to this idea of the future: what do you think will happen next with Rodarte?

LAURA: I don't think it's as simple as saying, "This is what the future holds." We want to broaden and evolve, but we take small steps in terms of growth because we're committed to developing a strong identity to how we do things and what our brand is. In terms of talking about the future, we're much more organic than that. I honestly couldn't tell you what is going to happen next. But that's what I like about it!

HUMBERTO: I think we share that organic approach to the future with Opening Ceremony. We're open to anything, so anything is possible! ◆

Rodarte sweatshirt and t-shirt photographed for Opening Ceremony. **RIGHT PAGE:** Rodarte FW11, photographed by Tim Barber for Opening Ceremony. **FOLLOWING SPREAD:** Opening Ceremony Resort '12, photographed by Tim Barber. **PAGES 334–337:** Opening Ceremony SS12, photographed by Tim Barber.

2012 KOREA : SEOUL

KUKJE GALLERY
A PLACE TO DISCOVER NEW ARTISTS.
54 SAMCHEONG-RO, JONGNO-GU
kukje.org

GOPCHANG JEONGOL
A DIVE BAR WHERE YOU CAN LISTEN TO SOME OLD K-POP AND FOLK MUSIC.
327-17 SEOKYO-DONG, MAPO-GU

GAEMIJIP
GOOD FOR THEIR HOME-MADE RICE ALCOHOL AND KIMCHI, WHICH ARE DISPLAYED IN JARS BELOW THE FLOOR.
528-4 SHINSA-DONG, KANGNAM-GU.

DONGDAEMUN MARKET
THE LARGEST SHOPPING MARKET IN TOWN! THERE ARE ALSO YOUNG, INDEPENDENT DESIGNERS REPRESENTED HERE. DON'T FORGET TO EAT THE STREET SNACKS, LIKE OUR FAVORITE DDUK-BOKKI (A SPICY KOREAN RICE CAKE).
JONGNO-6 GA 289-3, JONGNO-GU
dongdaemun.com

SANHO JEONBOK
A POPULAR RESTAURANT THAT GRILLS TRADITIONAL KOREAN PANCAKES TO ORDER!
1206 SAMDO 2-DONG, SEJU-DO

OC Introduces Rodarte

From Berkeley buddies to long-term collaborators, Kate and Laura Mulleavy have been part of Carol and Humberto's story from the beginning. When Rodarte launched in 2005, Opening Ceremony was one of the very first to recognize the unique vision. Based in their native Pasadena, California, Kate and Laura have worked outside the fashion establishment since their company's inception. They are continually inspired by farflung references in film, art, science, literature, and pop culture, and are apt to reference anything from American 60s and 70s land art to classic Disneyana. In the past few years, the Mulleavys have taken their creative vision beyond fashion, designing ballet costumes for Darren Aronofsky's 2011 film *Black Swan*, and showing their design work at MOCA Los Angeles and the Cooper-Hewitt National Design Museum in New York. 2011 also saw the debut of their limited-edition, two-season collection in collaboration with Opening Ceremony. With their deeply personal aesthetic and true curiosity about the world, Kate and Laura are a continual inspiration.

OPENING

CEREMONY

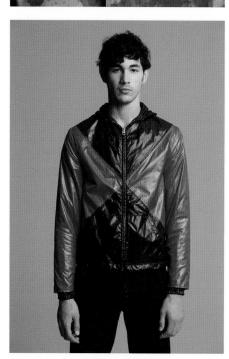

Opening Ceremony
men's FW12,
photographed by Todd
Jordan. PREVIOUS
SPREAD: Opening
Ceremony men's SS12,
photographed by Todd
Jordan. FOLLOWING
SPREAD: Opening
Ceremony women's
FW12, photographed
by Todd Jordan.

We were so proud to be appointed creative directors at Kenzo, opening a new chapter in our story!

Kenzo SS12, photographed by Ludwig Bonnet (Java Fashion). RIGHT PAGE, TOP: Humberto and Carol outside Kenzo; BOTTOM: Kenzo SS12, photographed by Ludwig Bonnet (Java Fashion). FOLLOWING SPREAD: Kenzo men's FW12, photographed by Patrice Stable (Studio Milpat).

In August 2011, Humberto and Carol were named creative directors of Kenzo, the storied Parisian brand founded by Japanese designer Kenzo Takada in 1970. As a Japanese designer in Paris, Kenzo brought an inclusive and bright diversity to ready-to-wear and beyond, with indelible ideas such as his wild "Jungle Jap" retail concept. This exuberance in fashion and love of internationalism is echoed by Opening Ceremony, so the pairing felt instantly appropriate. Carol and Humberto's first show with Kenzo for Spring 2012 was staged at the Paris headquarters on rue Vivienne. Truly a family affair, the show featured live music orchestrated by Jason Schwartzman and closed with Chloë Sevigny in a blue jumpsuit, all of it filmed by Spike Jonze for a short documentary. The collection's inspiration drew from Ellsworth Kelly's primary colors and the souvenirs of seaside towns, translated into fishnet-printed primary separates, bold reversible taffeta dresses and palazzo pants, and inventively netted handbags and boater hats. Bringing the same enthusiasm and creativity to Kenzo as they have for ten years at Opening Ceremony, Carol and Humberto have placed their brightly colored flag on the 2nd arrondissement of Paris.

345

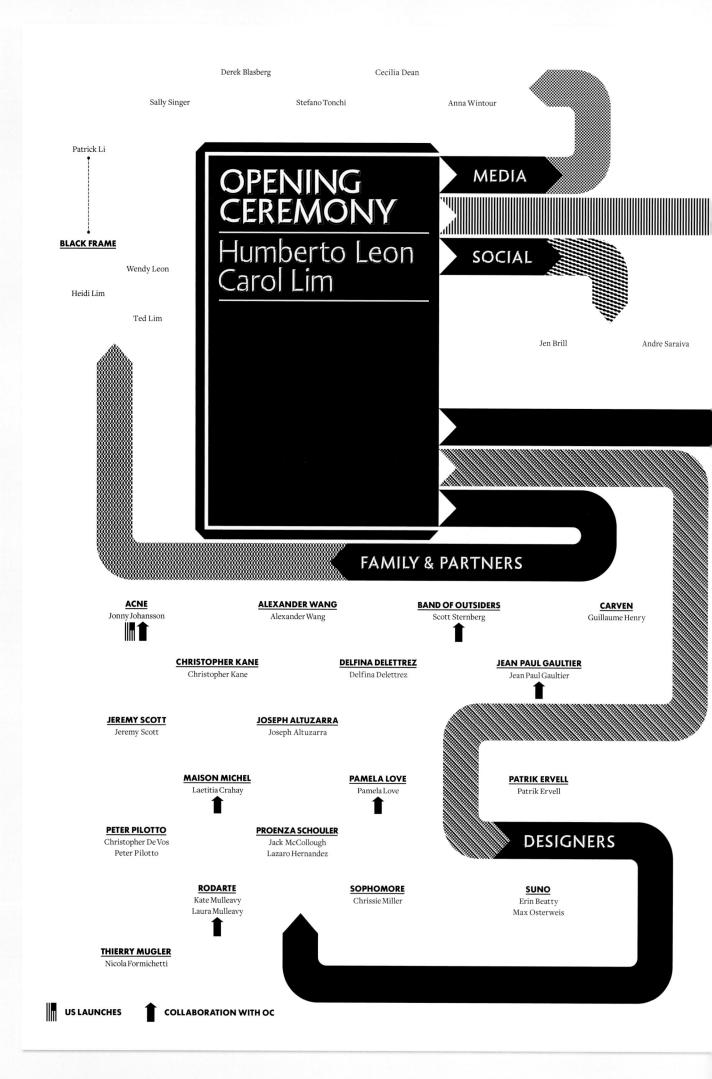

Derek Blasberg   Cecilia Dean

Sally Singer   Stefano Tonchi   Anna Wintour

Patrick Li

OPENING CEREMONY
Humberto Leon
Carol Lim

MEDIA

SOCIAL

BLACK FRAME

Wendy Leon

Heidi Lim

Ted Lim

Jen Brill   Andre Saraiva

FAMILY & PARTNERS

ACNE
Jonny Johansson

ALEXANDER WANG
Alexander Wang

BAND OF OUTSIDERS
Scott Sternberg

CARVEN
Guillaume Henry

CHRISTOPHER KANE
Christopher Kane

DELFINA DELETTREZ
Delfina Delettrez

JEAN PAUL GAULTIER
Jean Paul Gaultier

JEREMY SCOTT
Jeremy Scott

JOSEPH ALTUZARRA
Joseph Altuzarra

MAISON MICHEL
Laetitia Crahay

PAMELA LOVE
Pamela Love

PATRIK ERVELL
Patrik Ervell

PETER PILOTTO
Christopher De Vos
Peter Pilotto

PROENZA SCHOULER
Jack McCollough
Lazaro Hernandez

DESIGNERS

RODARTE
Kate Mulleavy
Laura Mulleavy

SOPHOMORE
Chrissie Miller

SUNO
Erin Beatty
Max Osterweis

THIERRY MUGLER
Nicola Formichetti

US LAUNCHES   **COLLABORATION WITH OC**

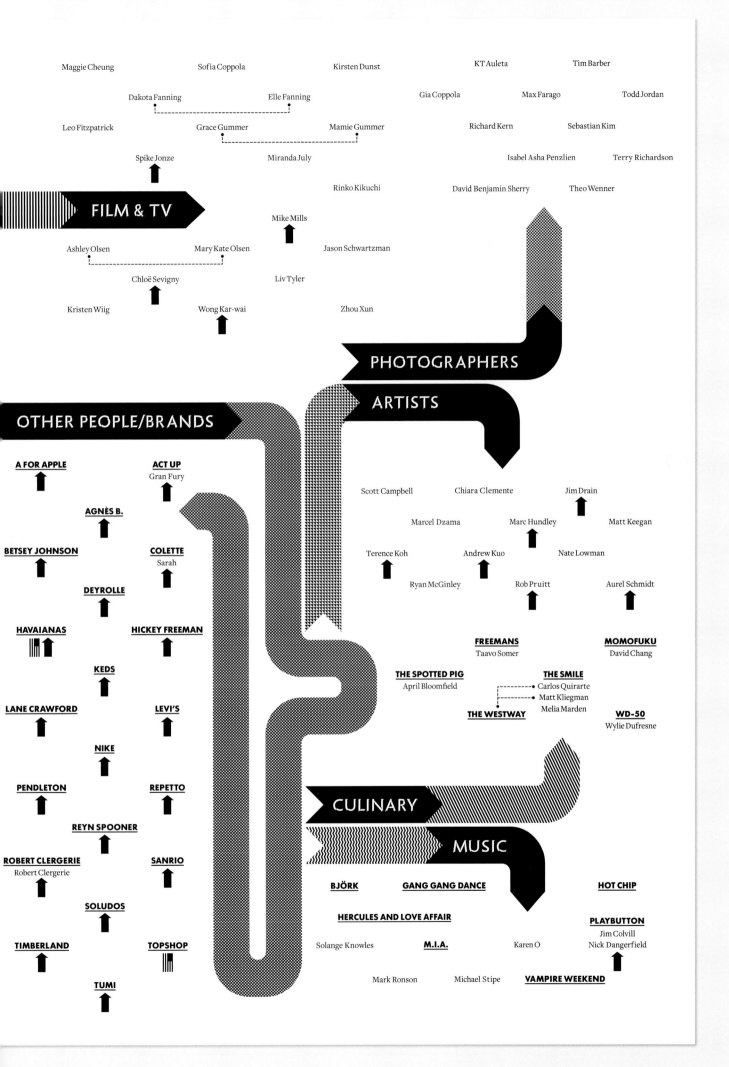

Maggie Cheung   Sofia Coppola   Kirsten Dunst   KT Auleta   Tim Barber

Dakota Fanning   Elle Fanning   Gia Coppola   Max Farago   Todd Jordan

Leo Fitzpatrick   Grace Gummer   Mamie Gummer   Richard Kern   Sebastian Kim

Spike Jonze   Miranda July   Isabel Asha Penzlien   Terry Richardson

Rinko Kikuchi   David Benjamin Sherry   Theo Wenner

FILM & TV

Mike Mills

Ashley Olsen   Mary Kate Olsen   Jason Schwartzman

Chloë Sevigny   Liv Tyler

Kristen Wiig   Wong Kar-wai   Zhou Xun

PHOTOGRAPHERS

ARTISTS

OTHER PEOPLE/BRANDS

A FOR APPLE

ACT UP
Gran Fury

AGNÈS B.

Scott Campbell   Chiara Clemente   Jim Drain

Marcel Dzama   Marc Hundley   Matt Keegan

BETSEY JOHNSON

COLETTE
Sarah

Terence Koh   Andrew Kuo   Nate Lowman

DEYROLLE

Ryan McGinley   Rob Pruitt   Aurel Schmidt

HAVAIANAS

HICKEY FREEMAN

FREEMANS
Taavo Somer

MOMOFUKU
David Chang

KEDS

THE SPOTTED PIG
April Bloomfield

THE SMILE
Carlos Quirarte
Matt Kliegman
Melia Marden

LANE CRAWFORD

LEVI'S

THE WESTWAY

WD-50
Wylie Dufresne

NIKE

PENDLETON

REPETTO

CULINARY

REYN SPOONER

MUSIC

ROBERT CLERGERIE
Robert Clergerie

SANRIO

BJÖRK   **GANG GANG DANCE**   **HOT CHIP**

SOLUDOS

HERCULES AND LOVE AFFAIR

PLAYBUTTON
Jim Colvill

TIMBERLAND

TOPSHOP

Solange Knowles   **M.I.A.**   Karen O   Nick Dangerfield

TUMI

Mark Ronson   Michael Stipe   **VAMPIRE WEEKEND**

Sally Singer photographed
by Terry Richardson, 2011.
PREVIOUS SPREAD: Chart
by Patrick Li, 2011.

This Is Magnificent

SALLY SINGER

Sally Singer is the editor-in-chief of T: The New York Times Style Magazine. *Prior to joining* The Times, *she was the fashion news/features director of* Vogue *for eleven years. Singer has written for* New York *magazine,* The Atlantic Monthly, The Guardian, *and* The Economist, *among other publications.*

When Humberto approached me about writing about our alma mater, the University of California at Berkeley, and to what extent I felt it had influenced our careers and those of our fellow alums (the Mulleavy sisters of Rodarte fame, photographer Todd Selby, designers Patrik Ervell and Patrick Li), I must confess I was a tad baffled. "No idea," was my first response. And then I happened to be back in Berkeley, trudging up Telegraph Avenue toward Bancroft and Sproul Plaza, past the pizza slicers, the one remaining CD store, the sweatshirt dealers, and the head shops. How on earth could this place have nurtured a small pack of style obsessives? It made no sense.

But I *am* obsessive. So after not a few mental hikes through my memories of Berkeley, I think I have a slim grasp of how such a funny, messy place could have given birth to the globally chic crew at Opening Ceremony.

First, there is the issue of who goes to Cal (as the school is called). You get to go there, for the most part, because in high school you're smart in very straightforward ways: you test really well; you get really good grades. It's not because you're polished yet adorable, or have spent your summers racking up CV-stuffer internships, or know people who know people, or are in any way well-rounded or well-adjusted. You are probably just goofy smart, with all the attendant geekiness and sense of alienation that can bring. So you've probably suffered, turned inward a bit, and developed a pretty thick skin. You know who you are, whether you like yourself or not. You may have even spent some time considering how clothes could either conceal or dramatize your inner nerd-dom. This is all good.

Then there's the experience of being a student there, which can be trying even for the heartiest of loners. There's not a clique you want to join, not an established subculture worth wheedling into. Your lecture courses have maybe 2,000 other students in them, all trying to outwit the bell curve. Your discussion groups are attended by people you never see outside of the classroom. ("Where have they materialized from and where do they disappear to afterward," you ask.) You read

for yourself. You study for yourself. You compete with yourself. And you live in your own head. This is also really good.

Then there's the brief encounter: you see someone who looks intriguing across a room, plaza, coffee shop, or BART platform, and you have to reach out in the moment or they'll be gone, lost in the misty afternoons of the Bay Area. You may never see them again. So you have to be intuitive, quick, sure of your taste, knowingly impulsive, socially proactive. This is darn hard but good.

Later, when these strange figures become your pals, you have to accept and find beauty and style where it resides locally. You walk through eucalyptus groves. You sit in gardens full of overgrown fuchsia trees. You shop for Japanese eggplants at the Berkeley Bowl and ponder the significance and diversity of aubergine. This is super good.

Whether this was all true for Humberto and Carol when they went to Cal, or whether it was only partially true, I can't say. And yet, when I think of my fellow Berkeley-ites, I think of their fierce intelligence, creative autonomy, an eye for sympathetic and surprising collaborators, and a sense of wonder in the face of beauty in all its many forms. These are not people who were educated to look right or left, because when they were at university there was no one to look at on their right or their left. Instead they look inward; they look outward; and they look ahead. This is magnificent. ◆

GRAPHIC DESIGN
Jonathan Lee
Naomi Otsu

EDITORIAL/ARCHIVING ASSISTANCE
Bettina Chin
Alice Newell-Hanson
Etienne Pham
Gillian Tozer

**PHOTOGRAPHY FOR OPENING
CEREMONY, THROUGHOUT**
Christelle De Castro
Steven Chu
Olivia Jade Horner
Matthew Kelly
Anna Mackenzie
Brayden Olson
Shannon Sinclair
Adam Sinding
Ackime Snow
Crystal Sohn
Gewet Tekle
Lyndsy Welgos

RETOUCHING
Anna Mackenzie
Gewet Tekle
Soña Z

**OCTV DIRECTION, UNLESS
OTHERWISE CREDITED**
Andinh Ha
Bruce Thierry Cheung

SPECIAL THANKS
Wendy Leon and the whole Leon family
Heidi Lim and the whole Lim family
Tim Barber
Derek Blasberg
Autumn Furr
Brian Phillips
Juliana Ribeiro   } Black Frame
Margo Schneier
Jen Brill
Patrik Ervell
Noelia Estrada
Natalie Farrey
Lazaro Hernandez
Shu Hung
Jonny Johansson
Olivia Kim
Terence Koh
Andrew Kuo
Cynthia Leung
Jack McCollough
Ryan McGinley
Kate Mulleavy
Laura Mulleavy
Daria Radlinski
André Saraiva
Mikael Schiller
Sally Singer
Alexander Wang
Eric Wilson
*and our most heartfelt thanks to the entire
Opening Ceremony team, past and present.*

KEN MILLER THANKS
JH, SH, LBM, and VM

RIZZOLI THANKS
Amoreen Armetta
Joe Davidson
Mandy DeLucia
Maria Pia Gramaglia
Colin Hough-Trapp
Kayleigh Jankowski
Daniel Melamud
Charles Miers
Lynn Scrabis

C is for Celebration!

BIRTHDAY

HAPPY B·DAY TASHI! 6/26/

OU ARE
EATED AT
LE NUMBER

OC FAMILY BONDING

CAVIAR

JOYCE, KATHY, DANNY, REGINA

LADIES NIGHT

At Opening Ceremony parties, we can actually play music that we love because people just want to have fun and dance. Everyone knows that Opening Ceremony throws the best parties.

HARLEY VIERA-NEWTON +
CASSIE COANE, DJS

GA   GA0 43
GEN ADM STANDING
THE BOWERY PRESE
YEAH YEAH YEA

OPENING CEREMONY

JIMMY, SHEA,

the OPENING CEREMONY

YOU ARE SEATED AT
TABLE NUMBER 21

PENDLETON ROUND UP
PENDLETON RODEO